## THE HYPNOTIC WORLD OF PAUL MCKENNA

Paul McKenna was a successful DJ for Capital FM and
Radio One, before leaving to follow his career
in hypnosis full-time.

At twenty-nine Paul McKenna is Britain's foremost
hypnotist. In addition to his bestselling self-help tapes,
he has his own popular stage show, which has now been
brought to television audiences by Carlton.

# The Hypnotic World Of

*Paul McKenna*

*faber and faber*

LONDON · BOSTON

First published in Great Britain in 1993 by
Faber and Faber Limited
3 Queen Square London WC1N 3AU

Phototypeset by Intype Ltd, London
Printed in England by
Mackays of Chatham PLC, Chatham, Kent

IMPORTANT

Do not follow the following induction techniques if you suffer from
epilepsy or clinical depression. It is NOT a substitute for medical or
psychiatric treatment. If in doubt, consult your doctor.

Illustrations © Max Ellis, 1993
Diagram 2 courtesy of the *Daily Mail*
with annotations by Nigel Andrews, 1993

A CIP record for this book is available from the British Library

ISBN 0-571-16802-7

10 9 8 7 6 5

To CLARE STAPLES,
who helped me write this book
and whose additional research
and input were invaluable

# Contents

# List of Plates

When Galileo developed the first astronomical telescope
he offered proof of new worlds.
However, no one would look through it,
and he was forced to renounce what we now all accept to
be the truth.

Today everyone looks to the stars,
but the new worlds are within us.

# Introduction

You hold in your hands a book containing esoteric knowledge – the strategies and techniques of history's most mesmeric characters. The pages that follow will reveal to you the secrets of hypnosis.

You might be reading this book because you are interested in becoming a stage hypnotist or a hypnotherapist. Or maybe you want to learn about some of the techniques I have found helpful when working with people as varied as business executives and Olympic athletes, helping them to achieve their goals. Or perhaps you are simply curious about the fascinating subject of hypnosis.

When you are hypnotized you can do the most amazing things. You can hallucinate enchanted kingdoms, animals and objects, and have imaginary conversations with historical figures. You can regress to any age and recall events long forgotten, writing and speaking as you did then. You can return to a 'previous life' and even go to a 'future life'. You can forget your name and your sex. You can undergo major surgery without any anaesthetic and feel drunk without touching a drop of alcohol. Some short-sighted people can have the shape of their eyeballs changed and their distance vision improved. A person's heartbeat can be made faster or slower, and the amount of blood circulating in any limb can be increased. You can use hypnosis to overcome life-long fears or phobias, to lose weight, to stop smoking or to have better sex. You can be made to laugh hysterically or become ecstatic upon command. You can even be hypnotized so that the tendon reflex that makes a leg jump when it is tapped is eliminated. The list is endless, and almost unbelievable, but after reading this book you will understand how some of these things are possible.

You don't need to know right now how you intend to use this book; simply enjoy reading it. If the subject is new to you, I suggest that you start reading with an air of benevolent scepticism and try out the ideas for yourself. Only then will you be able to understand the true power of hypnotism.

You do not need to have any previous knowledge of hypnosis to use the techniques described here. I have met plenty of people with an intellectual understanding of the subject who remain ignorant simply because they have never tried it for themselves. That is like reading a cookery book and talking about the recipes without ever cooking and tasting them.

Some excellent books on particular aspects of this fascinating subject already exist, but many of them are highly specialized and technical. This book is designed to give you a general overview of hypnosis. Knowledge is power: we live in an information age and the more information you have, the more choices you can make and the more powerful you are.

Hypnosis is a vast subject and has many specific applications, from therapy to entertainment, from business to sport. My approach here has been to outline the work of key individuals, each one a specialist in a particular field of interest.

The ideas I express in this book have developed from my own unique way of looking at the world. Understanding of hypnosis, though, is growing and deepening every year, and I hope that in ten years' time it will be possible to write a book on the advances made that goes even further than this one can today. Who knows – maybe by then you will have something to contribute to it?

It is important to remember that our beliefs and theories are only tools to help us understand reality. We must avoid becoming too attached to them, because we may need to change them in order to understand the world better.

As they start to use the following techniques, most people find that they somehow feel more in control of their lives. After reading this book, I hope that the world will become a new playground for you and that you will have as much fun in it as I have had since I began applying hypnosis to my life and the way I live it.

Paul McKenna
LONDON, *March 1993*

# Acknowledgements

Thanks to an incredible therapist and friend, Hugh Willbourn.

Many thanks also to my colleague Michael Breen, whose expert knowledge and unique perspective has enriched my work and taught me so much.

And thank you to Tracey Scoffield, who had enough vision to see the bigger picture and get me to write this book in the first place; to Dr Chet Snow for permission to quote from his excellent book *Dreams of the Future*; and to Lesley Levene, who polished and corrected my manuscript into this book.

# The History of Hypnosis

I don't know about you, but the mere mention of the word 'history' usually puts me into a deep trance! Here, though, is a short, action-packed account, picking out the people whose work influenced me the most and made significant contributions to the development of our understanding of hypnosis.

The earliest references to hypnosis date back to ancient Egypt and Greece. Indeed, '*hypnos*' is the Greek word for sleep, although the actual state of hypnosis is very different from that of sleep. Both cultures had religious centres where people came for help with their problems. Hypnosis was used to induce dreams, which were then analysed to get to the root of the trouble.

There are many references to trance and hypnosis in early writings. In 2600 BC the father of Chinese medicine, Wong Tai, wrote about techniques that involved incantations and passes of the hands. The Hindu Vedas written around 1500 BC mention hypnotic procedures. Trance-like states occur in many shamanistic, druidic, voodoo, yogic and religious practices.

## HYPNOTIC PIONEERS

The modern father of hypnosis was an Austrian physician, Franz Mesmer (1734–1815), from whose name the word 'mesmerism' is derived. Though much maligned by the medical world of his day, Mesmer was nevertheless a brilliant man. He developed the theory of 'animal magnetism' – the idea that diseases are the result of blockages in the flow of magnetic forces in the body. He believed he could store his animal magnetism in baths of iron filings and transfer it to patients with rods or by 'mesmeric passes'.

The mesmeric pass must surely go down in history as one of the most interesting, and undoubtedly the most long-winded, ways of putting someone into a trance. Mesmer would stand his subjects quite still while he swept his arms across their body, sometimes for hours on end. I suspect that this probably had the effect of boring patients into a trance, but it was certainly quite effective.

Mesmer himself was very much a showman, conveying by his manner that something was going to happen to the patient. In itself this form of indirect suggestion was very powerful. Mesmer was also responsible for the popular image of the hypnotist as a man with magnetic eyes, a cape and goatee beard. His success fuelled jealousy among many of his colleagues and this eventually led to his public humiliation. Looking back, it is quite incredible that hypnosis survived these early years, because the medical world was so dead set against it.

Another forward thinker was John Elliotson (1791–1868), a professor at London University, who is famous for introducing the stethoscope into England. He also tried to champion the cause of mesmerism, but was forced to resign. He continued to give demonstrations of mesmerism in his own home to any interested parties, and this led to a steady increase in literature on the subject.

The next real pioneer of hypnosis in Britain appeared in the mid-nineteenth century with James Braid (1795–1860). Primarily a Scottish eye doctor, he developed an interest in mesmerism quite by chance. One day, when he was late for an appointment, he found his patient in the waiting room staring into an old lamp, his eyes glazed. Fascinated, Braid gave the patient some commands, telling him to close his eyes and go to sleep. The patient complied and Braid's interest grew. He discovered that getting a patient to fixate upon something was one of the most important components of putting them into a trance.

The swinging watch, which many people associate with hypnosis, was popular in the early days as an object of fixation. Following his discovery that it was not necessary to go through all the palaver of mesmeric passes, Braid published a book in which he proposed that the phenomenon now be called hypnotism.

Meanwhile, a British surgeon in India, James Esdaile (1808–59), recognized the enormous benefits of hypnotism for pain relief and performed hundreds of major operations using hypnosis as his only anaesthetic. When he returned to England he tried to convince the medical establishment of his findings, but they laughed at him and declared that pain was character-building (although they were biased in favour of the new chemical anaesthetics, which they could control and, of course, charge more money for). So hypnosis became, and remains to this day, an 'alternative' form of medicine.

The French were also taking an interest in the subject of hypnosis, and many breakthroughs were made by such men as Ambrose Liébeault (1823–1904), J. M. Charcot (1825–93) and Charles Richet (1850–1935).

The work of another Frenchman, Emile Coué (1857–1926), was very interesting. He moved away from conventional approaches and pioneered the use of auto-suggestion. He is most famous for the phrase, 'Day by day in every way I am getting better and better.' His technique was one of affirmation and it has been championed in countless modern books.

A man of enormous compassion, Coué believed that he did not heal people himself but merely facilitated their own self-healing. He understood the importance of the subject's participation in hypnosis, and was a forerunner of those modern practitioners who claim, 'There is no such thing as hypnosis, only self-hypnosis.'

Perhaps his most famous idea was that the imagination is always more powerful than the will. For example, if you ask someone to walk across a plank of wood on the floor, they can usually do it without wobbling. However, if you tell them to close their eyes and *imagine* the plank is suspended between two buildings hundreds of feet above the ground, they will start to sway.

In a sense Coué also anticipated the placebo effect – treatment of no intrinsic value the power of which lies in suggestion: patients are told that they are being given a drug that will cure them. Recent research on placebos is quite startling. In some cases statistics indicate that placebos can work better than many of modern medicine's most popular drugs. It seems that while drugs are not always necessary for recovery from illness belief in recovery is!

Sigmund Freud (1856–1939) was also interested in hypnosis, initially using it extensively in his work. He eventually abandoned the practice – for several reasons, not least that he wasn't any good at it! He favoured psychoanalysis, which involves the patient lying on a couch and the analyst doing a lot of listening. He believed that the evolution of the self was a difficult process of working through stages of sexual development, with repressed memories of traumatic incidents the main cause of psychological problems. This is an interesting *idea* that has yet to be proved.

Freud's early rejection of hypnosis delayed the development of hypnotherapy, turning the focus of psychology away from hypnosis and towards psychoanalysis. However, things picked up in the 1930s in America with the publication of Clark Hull's book, *Hypnosis and Suggestibility*.

In more recent times, the recognized leading authority on clinical hypnosis was Milton H. Erickson, MD (1901–80), a remarkable man and a highly effective psychotherapist. As a teenager he was stricken with polio and paralysed, but he remobilized himself. It was while paralysed that he had an unusual opportunity to observe people, and he noticed that what people said and what they did were often very different. He became fascinated by human psychology and devised countless innovative and creative ways to help people. He healed through metaphor, surprise, confusion and humour, as well as hypnosis. A master of 'indirect hypnosis', he was able to put a person into a trance without even mentioning the word hypnosis.

It is becoming more and more accepted that an understanding of hypnosis is essential for the efficient practice of every type of psychotherapy. Erickson's approach and its derivatives are without question the most effective techniques, and for that reason I will cover them in some detail later (see pages 147–153).

Over the years hypnosis has gained ground and respectability within the medical profession. Although hypnosis and medicine are not the same, they are now acknowledged as being related, and it is only a matter of time before hypnosis becomes a mainstream practice, as acceptable to the general public as a visit to the dentist.

## HYPNOSIS IN HISTORY

I have run through the main pioneers in the exploration and study of hypnosis, but it is also interesting that many creative individuals have used a trance-like state to access their talents. Artists, writers, poets and composers have induced a form of hypnotic trance to help them with their work.

The poet Alfred, Lord Tennyson (1809–92) would repeat his own name to himself again and again like a mantra, and by doing this would access a different state of consciousness in which whole poems came to him that he could then transcribe. Mozart (1756–91) apparently composed *Cosi fan tutte*, one of his most famous operas, while hypnotized, and Rachmaninov (1873–1943) reportedly composed one of his concertos following a post-hypnotic suggestion.

When the University of Strasbourg gave classes in hypnosis, students included the poet and playwright Goethe (1749–1832) as well as another composer, Chopin (1810–49). Thomas Edison (1847–1931), Nikola Tesla (1856–1943), Henry Ford (1863–1947), Albert Einstein (1879–1955) and Aldous Huxley (1894–1963) all used trance-like states to help in the development of their ideas.

Many of history's greatest innovators made documented use of some 'special' level of consciousness. These days huge numbers of leading athletes, business people and artists in many different fields use similar approaches with great success.

The Dalai Lama recently questioned our reasons for sending investigative teams into outer space and under the sea when the real undiscovered treasures of humanity lie within the realms of our minds, and I must say I have to agree with him!

# 2

# What is Hypnosis?

## THE HUMAN MIND

To understand what hypnosis is and how it works, you need to know something about your mind – in particular, what is meant by the conscious and unsconscious minds.

The human mind can be compared to an iceberg, with the visible tip being the conscious mind and the invisible mass, or larger part of the mind, being the unconscious mind.

### The Conscious Mind

When I talk about the conscious mind, I am referring to the little voice in your head, the one that right now is saying, 'Oh yes, that little voice!' This is the mind you actively think with all day long. It can hold only a handful of ideas and thoughts at any one time – which is why, for example, many people memorize numbers in small chunks, 1943609315 being easier to remember as 194 (first chunk), 360 (second chunk), 9315 (third chunk), because on average the conscious mind can retain only between five and nine discrete units of information at any one time.

The conscious mind is critical and analytical; it sorts information by noticing differences.

## The Unconscious Mind

The unconscious mind contains all your wisdom, memories and intelligence; it is your source of creativity. It regulates body-maintenance, and autonomic processes like breathing, blood circulation and tissue regeneration. The conscious mind cannot heal a cut or accelerate your heartbeat to the correct rate; the unconscious mind does. It is the seat of your emotions and directs nearly all of your behaviour. Everything that has ever happened to you and everything that you have ever imagined is stored as a multi-sensory recording in your unconscious mind. You can use hypnosis to tap into the unconscious mind and reveal details of incidents that happened many years before, all of which are filed away somewhere.

The unconscious mind works by association, by looking at something and seeing the similarities with a past event.

Of course, the words 'conscious' and 'unconscious' are only models for the way your mind works, but they are the best and easiest way to explain the complicated structure of the human brain. 'Consciousness' is not fixed in either the conscious or the unconscious; it is a spectrum of awareness.

My favourite metaphor for the conscious and unconscious minds is a darkened room with all sorts of objects littered about it (the unconscious) and a torch (the conscious) picking out details in the room, able to focus upon only a few things at any one time. Whatever the torch is shining upon will be brightly lit and visible, while the rest of the room is dark; although the rest of the room is still there, you cannot see it. In the same way, whatever your attention is focused on is uppermost in your consciousness and the rest of your memories and your wisdom are still there.

In one sense our lives are run mainly by our unconscious minds. We are largely unaware of our autonomic processes and thinking, and yet every single second our unconscious mind receives two million messages of sensory awareness. It would be impossible to process all that information consciously, so the unconscious sorts it and presents you with a summary of what is taking place. For example, when you are at a party, your unconscious is monitoring all the conversations that are taking place around you. Then, if somebody over the other side of the room says your name, suddenly you hear it. The unconscious mind sorted that piece of information and brought it to your conscious attention.

The unconscious can also delete information from our awareness. A friend of mine is a builder. At work he gets lots of little cuts on his hands but he doesn't notice them, because they would interfere with the job, so his unconscious keeps his attention on his work and literally anaesthetizes any pain.

The interaction between the conscious and unconscious minds is going on all the time, but how is it decided what information each individual should specifically focus upon? How is it sifted by the unconscious and presented to your conscious mind? The answer is programming.

## CHILDHOOD PROGRAMMING

Everything that happened to you between the time you were born and about the age of six, particularly moments of intense emotion, builds the foundations of your thinking and your behaviour for the rest of your life.

A child's mind is open, like a sponge, taking in all the stimuli in its environment. The mind absorbs everything it can in order to develop. Before the age of six a child doesn't know enough to be able to rely on its own judgement and reasoning; its critical faculty is undeveloped (a critical faculty is the ability to question, judge, analyse, criticize and, very importantly, compare). It is because children haven't developed this critical faculty that they are so innocent and can believe in things like Father Christmas or fairies. It is also why so many people end up the same as their parents, programmed by chance events, opinions and the superstitions of those around them, who were in turn programmed in their own formative years.

While the small child has not yet developed a critical faculty, in adults this faculty is partially or completely suspended when they are in a hypnotic trance. In a hypnotic trance you focus on just one thing, or on one thing at a time, rather than on several things at once, and this leads to fascination and absorption – a very different state from our waking consciousness, when we are constantly comparing and criticizing.

Quite simply, hypnosis is a state that allows excellent communication with the unconscious mind. So when a stage hypnotist tells hypnotized subjects that they are ballet dancers and subjects begin leaping about the stage, the suggestion has gone straight into their unconscious mind. With their critical faculties suspended, subjects, although often baffled, have no means of arguing against the suggestion. They cannot reason, 'You are just a hypnotist telling me to do this and I am not a ballet dancer'; they cannot evaluate the suggestion, having nothing to compare it with, so they have to act as if it were true. They have lost access to any evidence to the contrary.

Suggestions are the key to hypnosis. Charles Baudouin,[1] a famous French hypnotist, defines suggestion as 'a proposed or imposed idea, image or concept from an operator accepted by the mind of a subject'. Hypnosis evolved as a way of enhancing suggestibility, through language and psychological techniques.

The human mind has been likened to a computer and, to continue the analogy, hypnosis is a way of reprogramming the computer. When the critical faculty is quietened during trance, new ideas may be put to a person which result in new patterns of behaviour.

So what is this mystical thing called a trance?

## TRANCE

If you ask most people whether they have ever been in a trance they will answer 'No,' but they will be wrong. Every single one of us enters naturally occurring trance states all day long – day-dreaming, being engrossed in a book or even while driving a car.

The key to identifying trance states is in the fixation of attention, either internally or externally. Quite simply, trance is all about the focus of a person's attention. When a subject is hypnotized, this focus is highly concentrated by suggestion.

Television, for example, promotes a trance state. When watching, you forget about the room around you – the carpet, curtains, the furniture; your focus is the television. Something scary happens on the screen and you sit forward, tense up and get a burst of adrenalin. Quite simply, you plug your experience into that little box and, while you are engrossed, it becomes your reality.

Not all trance is detached and simple. Even a very sophisticated process can be performed in a trance. Have you ever driven for several miles and then not been able to remember that part of the journey? You are driving competently but suddenly, when somebody speaks or something catches your attention, you cannot remember what you were thinking about before. You were in a trance.

Trance is often described as an altered state of consciousness, but altered from what? The way I see it, we are all perpetually moving from one kind of consciousness to another. Your state of mind when operating a computer, say, is simply different from what it is when you are in a lift, or in the bath, or in the middle of an intense conversation.

So what's the difference between these natural trances that people go in and out of all day long and a hypnotic trance? The difference is that hypnosis is a deliberately induced trance. Other deliberately created and utilized trances are commonly found in disciplines such as yoga and meditation, and also in newer areas such as creative visualization and stress management.

The context for hypnosis is most typically a therapy session or a stage show where the hypnotist alters the subjects' awareness through language and psychological techniques. The hypnotist is the facilitator, the guide, elected by subjects for their journey through the realms of their consciousness.

The name given to the most extreme state of hypnosis is somnambulism. Somnambulist subjects have access to all the hypnotic phenomena; they are in a psychologically limitless environment. Subjects can regress to early childhood, transforming their manner and speech to those of a child, and can achieve all the traditional deep-trance phenomena that I will refer to in more detail later.

In a hypnotic trance the conventional limitations of the beliefs which determine everyday life do not exist. There is complete flexibility in the recovery of memories from your personal history. You are able to recall moments of trauma and gain new insights about them. You can tap into moments of personal excellence and replicate them in the future (athletes use this approach to reach peak perform-ance states, retriggering them at appropriate times). You can even go into the future, imagine skills and resources you would like to have and bring them back with you!

So, that's what a trance is. Now what does it feel like?

## The Experience of Trance

When you go into a trance, you will experience a change in awareness. Just as everybody is different in the way they experience life, so each person's way of experiencing trance is unique, and every trance may also be different. You could even say that there is no such thing as a trance state, only infinite altered states of consciousness.

In many cases naïve subjects do not actually believe that they have been hypnotized when they come out of a trance. This is often due to preconceptions about what trance will be like and then surprise when the experience does not match expectations. While hypnotized you do not necessarily stop being aware or conscious of what is going on around you; you are actually in a heightened state of awareness.

When people's consciousness is altered, they automatically experience certain changes. Although it would be very unusual for somebody to experience all of these, here are seven of the most common *internal* characteristics of a hypnotic trance state:

1   FIXATION   You become fascinated by an object or a train of thought, an idea, images or even your own breathing.

2   SENSORY CHANGES   Your sensory awareness alters:

sounds may appear louder and crisper, or quieter; feelings may be stronger or more dulled; colours may appear brighter or more hazy.

3   TIME DISTORTION   Your experience of time may change. It is common for an hour in trance to seem like five minutes.

4   EFFORTLESSNESS   Subjects often find ideas and images come and go without any effort on their part.

5   TRANCE LOGIC   Situations that could appear unusual or illogical in the waking state (existence of fantasy kingdoms, appearance of talking animals and historical figures) are more easily accepted and explored.

6   DIFFERENCES IN TIME AND SPACE   You can age and life-regress, or travel forward in time and space. You can even exist in two places at the same time. As in dreams, all events can be happening now – past, present and future occurring simultaneously.

7   AMNESIA   It is very likely that you will be unable to remember all of what happened during your trance. In most cases your recall will be at best partial, and it may well also be unclear, disordered and without much detail.

That's how it feels when you are in a trance, but there are also certain sensory signals hypnotists can use to tell them that a subject's awareness is altering. Once again everyone is unique, but here are the most common *external* signals.

1   MUSCULAR CHANGES   A trance state can be one of relaxation. Often muscles become limp and loose, or they may even twitch. It becomes more obvious, for

example, if a subject is someone who normally has a fixed grin or scowl. The face becomes relaxed and in some cases the lower lip becomes bigger. Amazingly, there are over 180 muscles in the face that can be moved in isolation. A subject may begin to swallow more or less. The muscles may become tight and rigid as an individual goes into a trance during a state of excitement at, for example, a religious rally.

2  EYES  Many subjects close their eyes when going into trance. Some subjects display REMs (rapid eye movements), which can be seen behind the eyelid; this indicates a shift in brain waves.

When you are visualizing internally with your eyes closed, the hypnotist will be able to see eyeball movements behind your eyelids.

When subjects go into trance with their eyes open, the eyes often look glazed. There may be pupil dilation, and here the rule is simple: the more open an individual is, the more dilated their pupils will be. The eyes may roll upwards, beneath the eyelids. There may well be some de-focusing of the eyes when subjects are engaged in internal dialogue. The rate of blinking may also change.

3  SKIN COLOUR  There are often slight skin colour changes around the face, due to redistribution of blood. As muscular tension is relaxed, blood can flow in the capillaries closer to the surface of the skin.

4  BREATHING  There will almost always be a change in your breathing pattern as you go into a trance. Some people breathe faster, but the majority slow down

their breathing as they relax. The depth can change from shallow to deep, and often when subjects are visualizing they tend to breathe from their chest.

5   PERISTALSIS   Tension and stress arrest the digestion. As people relax the digestive system gets going again and I often hear the sound of peristalsis, or 'tummy rumbles', as my subjects go into a trance.

6   LITERALISM   Hypnotic subjects tend to think and speak more literally. For example, to demonstrate this point I once put my hand six inches from a hypnotized subject's face and asked what was in front of him. He replied, 'Nothing', but when I asked him what was in front of that he said, 'Your hand.' That's a literal answer!

## DIFFERENT SCHOOLS OF THOUGHT

Having given this very brief introduction to the human brain, what a trance is, what it can feel like and the various hypnotic phenomena somebody in a trance manifests, the next thing to consider is just what hypnosis is. Rather than simply present you with my opinion, though, I'm going to outline a few different theories so you can draw your own conclusions.

Certain psychologists deny the existence of hypnosis altogether. They say that it is not a special state but a vestige of 'compliance behaviour', a culturally defined situation of influence. They argue that as subjects are merely obeying 'task-motivating' instructions in the waking state, those who are 'hypnotized' are just role-playing in context-dependent situations. They might behave like this for any number of reasons – because they are too embarrassed to do otherwise, because they want to please the hypnotist, because they actually believe in what they imagine or because they are playing the hypnotic role and must do what is expected of them. Psychologists like Sarbin compare hypnotized subjects to actors in that both lose themselves in a role to the exclusion of self-awareness.

They also claim that there is no simple scientific, psychological measure that proves a hypnotic state exists, because all of the phenomena exhibited by hypnotized subjects can also be found in the waking state. However, the fact that we cannot scientifically measure something does not mean it doesn't exist.

For the school of thought that sees consciousness as a spectrum, with no single threshold of trance and no unequivocal, clear-cut definition of waking consciousness, or measurable parameters, the same is true of hypnosis.

Professor Ernest Hilgard of Stanford University has worked hard over the years to bring greater respect to the study of hypnosis. He believes that through the hypnotic trance a separate part of the mind is contacted. He calls this the 'hidden observer'. The hypnotic induction supposedly enables subjects to cut themselves off from normal waking consciousness and contact this hidden observer or involuntary part of the mind. This can be done via automatic writing – a script produced involuntarily by, and in some instances without the conscious awareness of, the writer. You can also communicate with the unconscious mind through finger signals. In trance, you can ask your unconscious to choose a 'yes' finger and move it, then do the same for a 'no' finger. Next, just using questions to which the answer is 'Yes' or 'No', you can communicate through this channel, bypassing the conscious intellect.

Sigmund Freud studied and used hypnosis in his work and was probably the first proponent of the school of thought that said hypnosis allowed access to a separate, possibly more primitive, part of the mind. He compared the state of hypnosis with being in love: a person experiences the same compliance and absence of critical faculty; he saw the hypnotist as the beloved one and the relationship as an erotic tie. He also, however, saw a person's ability to be hypnotized as a sign of their psychological well-being.

Because of the sensory and awareness distortions reported by subjects which I described earlier, Martin Orne, a distinguished American psychologist, believes that hypnosis is a special state of consciousness. During his wide-ranging research, he became interested in what he calls 'trance logic'; for example, the ability to see the same person in two places simultaneously. Orne first came across 'trance logic' when he was trying to devise a test to differentiate between people genuinely in a trance and people simulating trance. He took each subject into a room and sat them down, placing a chair directly in front of them. Then he told them that the room was completely empty and asked them to walk across it. The simulators stood up, walked forward – and crashed into the chair! The people genuinely in a trance stood up and walked across the room, swerving to avoid the chair. When they were asked why they had swerved, they replied, 'To avoid the chair.' When he then asked, 'How come you saw the chair when I told you the room was empty?' they replied, 'What chair?'

Orne went round this illogical loop several times before deciding that such thinking was another hypnotic phenomenon: the ability of a hypnotic subject to hold simultaneously two contradictory beliefs, or to perceive simultaneously two incompatible perceptions. I had a fascinating example of this once at one of my shows. I had hypnotized a subject so that she would hallucinate all the men in the audience naked. She was enjoying looking around, so I asked her if any particular man caught her fancy. 'Oh yes,' she replied, grinning, 'that guy in the white shirt!' She could see him naked and with his shirt on at the same time.

Another theory sees hypnosis as an 'occult' practice, like astral projection, in which an individual's soul leaves his or her physical body. This idea is common in many cultures – think of the trances associated with so many different ancient magic and religious ceremonies. When spiritualist mediums 'channel', supposedly allowing another spirit to speak through them, they go into a trance to facilitate the process. One could argue from a hypnotic point of view that they are actually bringing out projections from their unconscious mind, in the same way that the 'hidden observer' is contacted.

Milton Erickson believed that the hypnotic state was just one of many naturally occurring states; it was integral to the individual and had nothing to do with role-playing. This line of argument sees hypnosis as a powerful psychological tool that allows a hypnotist to shape attention and ways of thinking by using a subject's own patterns of experience.

Researchers have gone to enormous lengths to investigate hypnosis in ever greater detail. Although as yet no definitive theory has emerged that satisfies all investigators, at the same time there have never been so many competent practitioners of hypnosis. For many people, especially those who have benefited from it, this academic disagreement doesn't matter. You don't need to be a mechanic to know how to drive a car. The phenomenon called hypnosis is happening every day all around us and you don't need letters after your name to be able to use it safely and efficiently.

## COMMON MISCONCEPTIONS

If experts cannot agree about just what hypnosis is, no wonder misconceptions abound. Let's try and clear up a few now.

Here are some of the most popular misconceptions:

1   HYPNOSIS CAN CURE ANYTHING   The truth is that hypnosis is not a blanket panacea. As is only to be expected, it doesn't always work for everything every single time. That said, though, I believe that it is undoubtedly the single most powerful and under-utilized resource in healthcare and personal development today.

2   HYPNOSIS IS IN SOME WAY ANTI-CHRISTIAN OR THE WORK OF THE DEVIL   According to *The*

*New Catholic Encyclopaedia*, the Catholic church (the largest Christian organization in the world) feels that 'Hypnotism is licit if used for licit purposes.'

It's interesting that while many Christian Scientists oppose hypnotism, the founder of their church, Mary Baker Eddy, became interested in spiritual healing after being cured of paralysis by a hypnotist.[2]

3   HYPNOSIS IS A MYSTERIOUS MAGIC POWER   Hypnosis is a series of established psychological techniques and language structures that anybody can learn. There is nothing supernatural or magic about it, and the fear that people have of hypnosis is simply a fear of the unknown. It is certainly true, though, that some of the beneficial effects could be described as magical.

4   ONLY WEAK-WILLED OR UNINTELLIGENT PEOPLE CAN BE HYPNOTIZED   As far as I am concerned, absolutely everybody can go into a trance. Circumstances, time, willingness of the subject and the competence of the hypnotist are all variable factors, but people are going into naturally occurring trances all the time.

5   PEOPLE WHO ARE HYPNOTIZED CAN BE MADE TO DO ANYTHING, EVEN ACTS THAT ARE AGAINST THEIR WILL   Laboratory experiments have shown that a subject will comply only with suggestions that fit their moral and value systems. Of course, people can be persuaded or forced to do things that conflict

with their normal values through lies and deceit, but you don't need a hypnotist for that. Hypnosis cannot make moral people behave immorally. Sadly, there are immoral people in the world who behave badly, but don't blame hypnosis.

6   A SUBJECT CAN ENTER A HYPNOTIC TRANCE AND NOT WAKE UP   This is impossible! Even in the most unlikely event of the hypnotist being called away or even dying during an induction, the subject would simply drift into normal sleep or immediately awake.

7   HYPNOSIS IS DANGEROUS! ONLY SPECIALLY TRAINED DOCTORS SHOULD EVER BE ALLOWED TO HYPNOTIZE ANYONE   There has never been a death recorded specifically due to hypnosis. Doctors practise medicine; their expertise is in anatomy and physiology. Hypnotists practise hypnotism, which is essentially a skill of communication. I am, none the less, very pleased to see doctors finally accepting hypnosis as a valuable alternative therapy, dentists using it as an anaesthetic and psychiatrists using it instead of, or combined with, psychotherapy.

Certain countries have even stricter rules than Britain on hypnotherapy and in some legally you now need a licence to put someone into a trance. It is amusing to think that when two people make love they induce altered states in one another. As Richard Bandler has asked, does this mean that all the married people in these countries are going to have to become licensed hypnotists?[3]

8 HYPNOSIS WILL CAUSE YOU TO REVEAL HIDDEN SECRETS This is a fear commonly expressed by people who are worried about volunteering at my shows. They are afraid that while hypnotized they will say something they would not normally say. But hypnosis is not a truth drug, and it is actually just as easy to lie in a trance state as it is in a normal state. As I have said before, while hypnotized you know perfectly well what you are doing and saying, and will not do or say anything that contravenes your inner principles.

9 ONLY 30 PER CENT OF THE POPULATION CAN BE HYPNOTIZED One group of hypnotists devised the idea of hypnotizability scales. Having decided that certain kinds of behaviour were 'trance phenomena', they could then say that when someone exhibited such behaviour they were in a trance. They tried to hypnotize a number of people using the same induction each time and had a 30 per cent success rate.

Rather than seeing this as a demonstration of the hypnotizability of the general population, I see it as a demonstraiton of the flexibility of the population to respond to a rigid induction. I have enormous doubts about the whole notion of grading depths of trance by any sort of scale, my reason being that it is possible to find every single so-called 'trance phenomenon' in the waking state.

For example, forgetting somebody's name – that's amnesia, which is a 'deep-trance phenomenon'. Have you ever looked at your finger to find a cut you had not noticed? That's anaesthesia, another 'deep-trance phenomenon'. Have you ever been looking for your car keys, only to find that they were in front of you all the time? That's a negative hallucination – once again a 'deep-trance phenomenon'.

If I were to go into some of the incredible things that I have overheard people saying after just one of my shows, I could fill this book with mad theories. Hypnosis is one of those subjects that everyone thinks they are an expert on, whether they know anything about the subject or not.

# 3

# Trance Inductions

## THE COMPONENTS OF A SUCCESSFUL HYPNOTIC INDUCTION

When I first studied hypnosis and learned to induce hypnotic trance, I found it very useful to watch all sorts of other hypnotists and copy what they did. During a trance there's quite a lot going on, so I practised just one aspect at a time until I could do that really well and then moved on to the next.

At the most basic level there is only one hypnotic induction: one person says to another, 'Go into a trance'! But this message can be conveyed in countless ways . . .

As with anything, hypnotic induction can be learned easily if you break it down into small enough pieces. 'Chunking down', as it is called, is one of the most effective ways of approaching any exercise or task. Like many skills, the more you practise the better you get.

The best way to become a hypnotist is to master these small chunks, one at a time. As we all go into naturally occurring trance states every day, you can use hypnosis as a tool deliberately to alter your consciousness. When you use words and body language to create changes in someone's awareness, you are in effect hypnotizing them.

I like to describe hypnotists as amplifiers in a biofeedback circuit, as illustrated below.

Hypnotists feed back to subjects their observations of the subjects' own experiences, with a change of focus. This redirection of attention then alters their consciousness. As hypnotists state what they observe, the subjects continually have to change their awareness to verify. For example, as shoulder twitching is mentioned, their attention moves there. This continual altering of attention guided by hypnotists has a cumulative effect. It is particularly effective to draw attention to something outside the subjects' direct attention, like the weight of their feet on the floor or the gaps between your words.

To be a successful hypnotist you need to see what is going on with a subject on every level; all your senses must be concentrated on the subject. As I have said, there are over 180 muscles in the face alone and a lot of information can be read from each one. When hypnotists give the message 'Go into a trance', they use their sensory acuity to look for psychological responses to that request, and then amplify them.

So, if a subject offers muscular relaxation and a deepening of breathing, the hypnotist might suggest, 'As you notice your breathing deepening you can relax even further,' and might also deepen his or her own breathing.

*Rapport*

Another essential ingredient in performing a successful induction is an ability to create rapport. All good hypnotists and masters of influence do this.

Rapport is bonding, the ability to make others feel that you understand them. It comes through communication, which is another name for the interaction of energy between people.

The greater part of interpersonal communication is 'non-verbal'. In fact, the statistics from one psychological research project indicate that 55 per cent is body language, 38 per cent tone of voice (tonality) and only 7 per cent content, or the words themselves.[1] Once you know this you can appreciate the truth in the old adage, 'It's not what you say, but *how* you say it that counts.'

Think about it. You may well be saying 'Yes' to something while unconsciously shaking your head. You may well be telling someone you're not upset at all, clenching your fists tightly all the time you're doing it. Many people's attempts at communication are filled with these kind of contradictions. Even a seemingly simple phrase like 'thank you' can convey pleasure, annoyance, surprise, apathy – all largely conveyed through the tone of the speaker. Words are the bones of a message; body language and tonality are what flesh it out.

Establishing rapport is something that most people aim for, although few do so consciously and deliberately. It can be fostered through sharing common ground, or commonality. This doesn't mean that you can have rapport only with people who are like you, because in fact it is *perceived* likenesses that create rapport. You have probably heard it said that opposites attract, and on the surface there may be some truth in the idea. However, if you look further, say at a relationship in which a husband is dominant and extrovert in his manner and the wife introvert and subservient, you will notice that although their personalities may indeed be different, their core beliefs about what male and female roles in a relationship are likely to be the same.

When you watch two people who have rapport, one's gestures, patterns of eye contact and voice will match, or complement, the other's. Have you ever been in a conversation and noticed that your body posture is an exact mirror image of the other person's? You cross your legs and moments later they do the same. That is the key to rapport – mirroring by becoming like another person. The golden rule is: People like other people whom they *perceive* as being like themselves.

Masters of influence are all experts in creating rapport. However, it is important to differentiate between matching, which creates rapport, and mimicking. Matching is a form of communication that usually takes place outside conscious awareness. If you mimic someone, they will become conscious of it and may be offended.

Here's an example of how it works. If someone keeps stabbing their finger at me during a conversation, I might nod my head with each stab, thus keeping 'in sync' with the rhythm of his or her body movements. It's particularly effective to copy a person's body posture and breathing patterns. Another way to mirror somebody is through tone of voice. If they talk really fast, then go to their speed and talk really fast too. Have you ever noticed that some people talk very quietly, and don't usually appreciate those with loud voices? Go to their level and talk quietly as well. It helps to take on the quality of their voice tone as well. Some people have a squeaky voice, while others are more resonant. By doing this you are creating bonding with another person, using that remaining 55 per cent and 38 per cent of your communication. And your listener will be thinking to themselves, 'I can trust this person because they are just like me.'

In our culture most people naturally and instinctively try to find rapport with other people through words:

'Where are you from?'
'I'm from London.'
'That's nice. I've been there.'

However, this technique uses only a small proportion of our communicative range. What happens if the other person mentions something you don't know about? Language is obviously the least effective way of creating rapport, and yet it is what most people tend to try first.

The more ways you can find to feed back to people their own behaviour, the greater the rapport you will create. It's fun to be imaginative, though if someone is pacing up and down a room, it might not be appropriate for you to stride alongside! On the other hand, you could tap your finger in time to the footsteps – rapport really can be that imperceptible!

To create common ground between yourself and other people, you don't have to mirror everything about them. Mastering the art of rapport is simply learning to become like others. We all do this to some extent anyway, but experts do it consciously, and the person they are focusing on doesn't have any choice but to like them.

I was talking to a corporate trainer recently who gives a wonderful demonstration of this while at lunch with potential clients. She tells them that before the end of the meal at least three people will come to her table, believing that they know her. She makes this happen simply by mirroring people on other tables. Drinking at the same time as them, and using similar gestures, gets other people's unconscious minds believing that she is just like them and that maybe they know her, so they come to find out where they know her from.

## Pacing and Leading

Pacing is the process of recognizing and meeting the subject's expectations and experience. It is essentially the active creation of rapport. A simple, basic way of starting to pace someone is to get into a state of rapport and maintain it non-verbally – for example, by matching the subject's breathing rate. Leading is the process of guiding the subject to the state or experience the hypnotist wishes to offer, linguistically or simply by changing his or her non-verbal behaviour while it is entrained to the subject's.

For example, when I've been working with people who are depressed, I know there's no point telling them to cheer up or be happy. That is completely contradictory to their ongoing experience. So what I do is match them by mirroring their body posture, breathing, tone of voice and energy level, or lack of it. Then I subtly begin to make small changes, gradually raising my energy level. I am constantly looking for feedback as I make the changes. Rapport is dynamic, so I have to keep responding to the physiological messages offered to me by the client. Successful politicians, sales and advertising people as well as hypnotists all do this to some extent.

Have you ever been in a room where someone yawns or starts scratching their nose and very soon other people start yawning or scratching for no apparent reason? This is an example of unconscious leading. The yawners and scratchers follow someone else's lead, without really noticing or knowing why. A salesman once told me that his success was due to getting excited about his products because he believed that excitement was contagious. He was right!

So now you'll understand what I mean when I say that often when I work with a client I first get rapport by describing their immediate experience – that is, what they are seeing, feeling and hearing. 'You are sitting here, with your feet on the floor, looking at me and listening to my words. . .' The next step is to suggest where I want them to go: '. . . as you wonder how it is that you are going to go into a trance.' Or I get rapport through mirroring a client's body posture, breathing, gestures and voice tonality. Then I gradually put myself into a trance and, because we are in rapport, the subject will follow and match the changes in my physiology. I then withdraw myself at an appropriate moment, while suggesting that the subject continue.

A fellow hypnotist was at a party recently when an argument started between two people in the corner. They began shouting, then all of a sudden one of them took a swing at the other, so my colleague ran over to stop it. I don't know if you've ever tried to tell someone to calm down when they are shouting, but it's not easy. Trying to hold someone back when they are in full swing is even worse, because they tend to hit you next. However, the hypnotist instinctively shouted (matching their volume level), while grabbing one of them from behind, 'That's right. It's very important to make your point! You can shout and be angry, and you really say clearly exactly what he should do [gradually lowering his voice] so that there's no goddamn mistake [lowering his voice further so it was at normal level, and sitting him down] about explaining the whole thing properly.' The man who moments earlier was shouting and swinging his fists couldn't understand where his anger had gone.

This was a highly successful example of instinctive pacing and leading. The hypnotist was flexible enough to understand the other person's world at that moment. 'You can shout and be angry' matched his energy level and he changed his behaviour to get the alteration he wanted in the other person.

By the way, I am not suggesting that you go out tomorrow to resolve all the world's arguments like this; the ability to make such interventions safely comes from years of training and practise. But you can start practising right now. Have fun experimenting yourself. Get into conversations with people and gently mirror their posture, voice tone, speed of speech, gestures and breathing. After a short while, make some subtle changes and after a few minutes look to see if the other people have followed. If they don't, then simply return to pacing them and make the changes more subtle. If you attempt to lead someone who doesn't follow immediately, you just need to establish a greater rapport. The really wonderful thing about rapport is that you don't have to be from a particular social background or possess a degree in nuclear physics to create a bond between yourself and others. Whatever we do, we are communicating and interacting all the time; rapport is a tool that gives you instant access to others.

*Rhythms*

There are natural rhythms in the way people talk, so a skilled hypnotist will match the rhythms of his or her speech with the subject's breathing cycle, while at the same time scanning for physiological feedback. Hypnotists observe their subject's breathing by looking at their face, or perhaps noticing the rise and fall of their shoulders. Hypnotists' behaviour is initially driven by their subjects. They match their speech to their clients' breathing by stressing the words at the top or bottom of the breathing cycle. For example,

                (*breath in*)
                **listening**                            **are**
          here        to                      you
      sit               me             how
    you              and      exactly
**As**                 **wondering**
                (*breath out*)

                **and**
going            trance    really
     to           a         enjoy
    relax   into          that
       **now**                wonderful

     **many**             **on**
   so      ways          is
   in      while     awareness
feeling         some   your
           of

Once hypnotists have matched the speed of their sub-jects' breathing, they can slow down the pace of their speech. Using this technique alone, expert hypnotists can take a subject in and out of trance purely by changing the speed and the stresses in their voice.

Many people wonder why hypnotists talk in a slow, mon-otone when performing an induction. Now you know! Good hypnotists will start speaking at a normal speed, but will slow down their speech and breathing as they lead their subjects into trance. I usually slow down to       about
30          per          cent          of
my                  normal              speed
of              speech
as                  I
induce                      trance.

While all this is taking place, hypnotists are selecting from the responses they are getting from the subject those that go towards the target state of trance. They reinforce and amplify these responses. For example, if a hypnotist suggests that the client can imagine walking on a beach and sees micro–muscular movements of the legs, that is a good indication that the subject is responding to the suggestion. A simple affirmative comment, such as 'Yes, that's right, just carry on just like that', is enough to enhance the experience.

It is also important to incorporate stimuli in the environ-ment. If an aeroplane flies overhead, rather than letting it become a distraction, the hypnotist might say, 'As you hear the sound of the aeroplane, that awareness sweeps through you taking you deeper.' By mentioning something, the subject's awareness is drawn to it. If the hypnotist were to say, 'Don't think of the aeroplane', the subject would then think about it and be confused, or even distracted from the possibilities of absorption in trance. The key is to use every element of the environment to build the subject's trance experience. If a distraction crops up, I will incorporate it in order to take the subject deeper into trance.

Noticing and using everything is the key to successful inductions. When I am working with a subject who laughs while going into trance, I use it. I pace and lead; I laugh too. 'Yes, that's right, you can laugh, as you let that laughter release any tensions you had and prepare really to let go even further into trance.' The more flexible and responsive a hypnotist is to the subject, the more effective the induction.

## Transition

This is the next stage in a successful induction. It is a linguistic tool that allows the hypnotist to match a subject's ongoing experience while moving smoothly to an altered state, or trance. Words such as 'and', 'as', 'because', 'while' and 'when' are linguistic bridges and can be used to take a person deeper into trance.

For example, 'You've been listening to my words *and* relaxing further.' The first part of the sentence is matching the subject's direct experience, feeding back what is actually taking place; 'relaxing further' is the suggestion the hypnotist tags on to the true statement of what he or she wants to have happen next. There is really no logical connection between listening to words and relaxation, but if you join them with 'and' it appears that there is.

A large part of hypnotic language consists of these transitions, and the technique is simple. The hypnotist describes something the subject can see, hear or feel, then links that by use of a transitional word to what the hypnotist wants to happen next. For example,

> 'You can feel the weight of your feet on the floor *while* you begin to notice the slightest changes *as* your eyelids blink *because* you know this is the only trance happening for you now.'

Hypnotists get a lot of their suggestions by just feeding back to the subject what they observe. For example, 'As you listen to me, letting your body twitch and your tummy rumble.' They imagine how subjects might look when they are in trance, using the signs described earlier, then use that picture to generate the ideas for the suggestions to move them towards the target state.

## Focus

Many people associate the idea of trance with having an inward focus of attention. Therefore it is most effective to give internally oriented suggestions. For example, 'Going deeper, inside yourself, to that resourceful place.' In this way the hypnotist redirects the subject's fixation or focus of attention.

Focus can be described as whatever you fix your attenton on. One of the golden rules of hypnosis has to be: You get more of what you focus on. This simple but important idea runs throughout the book.

Focus is what that old traditional tool of the hypnotist, the swinging watch, is all about. But focus can be fixed just as easily on a concept as an object. Through words the hypnotist conveys ideas that guide the focus of attention. When subjects introvert their attention, they have less left for external sensory stimuli as the hypnotist's words paint pictures in their mind.

*Framing*

In much the same way that photographers create the meaning of their pictures by deciding on what to put in and what to leave out of the frame, so the meaning of everything in our lives depends upon our frame of perception. The success of any hypnotic induction also depends upon the frame of perception. When people come to see my show they either expect to be hypnotized or to see someone else hypnotized. However, if I just walk up to a man in the street and tell him I am going to hypnotize him whether he likes it or not, I might get a very different response. The reason is that the same activity (hypnosis) has been placed in a different context.

In order to understand this fully you need to grasp a fundamental concept that runs throughout hypnosis: There is no meaning fixed in anything in life; meaning is always affected by your point of view. One of the main ways you create meaning is by the frames you choose to use, the context that you create. You decide how you perceive life: a glass of water can be half full or half empty, depending upon your personal frame of perception. Many of the meanings in your life are culturally embedded and derive from your parents' values.

Often the hypnotist will reframe something to create a different way of perceiving, giving it another interpretation. Think of advertisers. They know this because their job is essentially to frame certain products in the best possible light and they often do so by creating the idea that what they are selling will make you, or your life, better.

Many jokes are reframes. There are two horses standing in a pub and one says to other, 'What are you having?' The other replies, 'I'll have a pint of lager.' There's a dog behind them who says, 'If you are going to the bar, can you get me a bag of crisps while you're there?' The horses turn to each other and say, 'Good grief, a talking dog!'

Anything in life can have as many meanings as you create. Someone speaking loudly to you is fine in a noisy bar, but is altogether different and probably embarrassing in a library. 'The tall man stepped from the bushes and shot him . . .' sounds unpleasantly violent until we add, 'but unfortunately his camera didn't have any film in it.'

I believe that failure is an attitude rather than an outcome, and is determined by the way you frame things. For example, after Edison's seven-hundredth unsuccessful attempt to invent the electric light, he was asked by a *New York Times* reporter, 'How does it feel to have failed seven hundred times?' The great inventor responded, 'I have not failed seven hundred times. I have not failed once. I have succeeded in proving that those seven hundred ways will not work. When I have eliminated the ways that will not work, I will find the way that will work.'

Several thousand more experiments later, Edison finally found the one that would work and invented the electric light.[2]

You don't need hypnosis to do a reframe, but framing and reframing can be incredibly powerful in hypnosis, because when a subject is in trance, their critical faculties are quietened and they are able to consider more possibilities. In hypnotherapy the therapist will often get a client to look at a situation differently by reframing the context of the problem or the specific content.

To take an example between a therapist and client:

CLIENT: I'm just too scared to make the first move. There is someone I am really attracted to, but I'm so shy, I don't know what to say.

THERAPIST: What do you think it is that you are scared of?

CLIENT: I'm scared I will make a fool of myself. I'm sure I'll blush or get tongue-tied or something.

THERAPIST: Well, what do you have to offer to this person? Do you really care for them?

CLIENT: I'd like to! Yes, I really am serious. It really means a lot to me.

THERAPIST: And how can you show that?

CLIENT: Well, unless I can ask them out I guess I can't. But I'm too scared to do it.

THERAPIST: Well, maybe there is a way. You see, you can show them how much you care by being prepared to take a risk. . .

CLIENT: Uh?

THERAPIST: It may just be that the most attractive thing you can offer that person is your willingness to be embarrassed.

In this way the therapist shows the client how what they thought was their problem could be the beginning of their solution.

As I have already said, the success of an induction depends upon the frame within which it is set. Once when I was to give a demonstration of hypnosis on television I met with a potential problem. The audience from which I was going to draw my volunteers were in their late teens, far too 'cool' to let some guy get them doing silly things in front of their friends. Just before we went on to the air the compere introduced me to the studio audience by saying, 'This is Paul McKenna, and he's going to hypnotize some of you in a moment.' Fifty people then turned to look at me, as if to say, 'Oh yeah? Let's see you then, mate!'

It could have been a disaster: we would be on the air in a few minutes and at this rate I was going to have no volunteers, and therefore no show, live on television. I had to find a way to make the situation seem less threatening to the audience and turn it into something attractive that they really wanted to be involved in. I looked at them and said, 'You know in our culture a lot of people drink alcohol and take drugs to change the way they feel. Hypnosis is amazing because it is a *natural* state-changer. You could say it's a natural high.' Then, as an added bonus, I said, 'Some people even find it makes them better dancers as well.'

There was almost a stampede as they all eagerly volunteered. I had simply reframed the situation for them, set hypnosis in a new, desirable context, and yet at the same time I was still telling the truth. This is one of the basics, common to all good sales people – they look at their customers' needs and match them to their services.

One of my favourite examples of setting a brilliant frame comes in the form of a letter from a college student to her parents.

Dear Mum and Dad

Apologies for taking so long to write, but my writing utensils were destroyed in the fire at my flat. I am out of the hospital and the doctor says that I should be able to lead a normal healthy life. A handsome young man called Pete saved me from the fire and kindly offered to share his flat with me. He is very kind and polite and from a good family, so I think you'll approve when I tell you that we got married last week. I know you'll be even more excited when I tell you that you are going to be grandparents very soon.

Actually there wasn't a fire, I haven't been in hospital, I'm not married and I'm not pregnant, but I did fail my maths exam and I just wanted to make sure that when I told you that you put it in a proper perspective.

Love

Your daughter

The most powerful person in any group is the one who is most flexible. The individual with the most choices is the one who has most ways of looking at things and hence the greatest scope for control. Learning to use reframing is learning to increase your opportunities, which increases your flexibility, which increases your power.

Just acknowledging that a trauma is in the past and has ended is in itself a powerful and very healing reframe. Many high achievers do not regard things that happen to them as disasters or tragedies and instead always frame them as challenges or even opportunities. They achieve this by asking themselves, 'How does this help me?'

In order to answer this question you have to look at the particular situation in a different way, putting it in a positive context. It doesn't matter whether your new assessment is 'true' as long as you become empowered. Some people work as hard on their unhappiness as others do on feeling good, building up a view of life that says they are victims. This seems to me an unfortunate waste of energy, to say the least!

When you reframe a situation you give yourself more choices. Think back and remember some of the mistakes you have made, then consider for a moment what you have learned from them. Here's one benefit for a start. One of my favourite stories in this context comes from the man who started IBM, Tom Watson Snr, who said that if you want to double your success rate you first have to double your failure rate. All of a sudden mistakes take on a new meaning.

If you don't take responsibility for the frames you make

in your life, then someone else will. Advertisers, politicians, religions and others are all placing their products, services or views of how we should lead our lives in contexts that make them appear sophisticated, sexy, the right thing to do, worthy or desirable.

We all know of people who can frame anything to reveal doom and gloom. One of my clients had a fear of success which evolved from something his mother had told him as a child. He had said to her that when he grew up he wanted to be successful, and she had promptly replied that he didn't want to be successful because successful people had heart attacks. Of course, there is no logic in that statement, but as a child he couldn't know that. It was years later, looking back from his adult viewpoint and seeing the idea had no validity, before he could reframe it and put it in a new context: his mother had been trying to protect him with her limited knowledge at the time. For every negative belief there is a flip-side positive frame.

When I began working in the area of stress control with corporations, I noticed that some people thought this was a fad for executives only. I created a different frame for my stress-control work to give it more value by explaining how stress-control training not only enhances what you already do well, to enable you to do it even better, but also means you are likely to lengthen your life!

Looking at things in the context of your life can bring about all kinds of revelation. Sometimes I suggest to subjects that they imagine going to the end of their life, looking back and asking themselves what they wish they done more of and what they wish they had done less of. The answers people tend to give are that they wish they had loved more, laughed more and worried less. This perspective can be transformational – I recommend you to try it. You will find a trance technique specifically for this in the self-hypnosis section (pages 120–135).

## Waking Up

No one has ever failed to wake up from a trance. We know that if anything unfortunate were to happen to the hypnotist the subject would awake. There are three ways to come out of trance. First, by responding to a hypnotic command or request to awaken; second, by falling into ordinary sleep and waking naturally from that; and third, by waking spontaneously.

Hypnotists normally wake up their subjects at the end of the trance by straightforward instruction, or by just gradually raising their voice. For example,

'As I count backwards from five to one you will wake up refreshed, relaxed and alert, filled with an inner sense of optimism. Five, coming back. Four, beginning to wake up. Three, that's good. Two, and you're beginning to discover what an eye-opening experience trance is. One, you are wide awake!'

Some subjects awake refusing to believe they were in trance at all, even though the hypnotist was able to see many psychological indications that they had moved into an altered state of consciousness. In fact, audiences often hear the most active and entertaining hypnotic subjects in my show swear blind they have not been hypnotized and have been on stage only five minutes. When subjects don't know that they have been in trance, this is normally because their expectations of trance did not exactly match their experience of it. If their preconceptions about what was going to happen and what actually did happen do not match, they are led to the false conclusion that they were not hypnotized, so their friends have to tell them what's happened. Well, maybe that's what friends are for!

For some strange reason, a lot of people think that they will not be able to hear anything when they are in a trance and so, when they continue to hear the hypnotist talking, they believe they are still completely conscious. This applies equally to thinking: you still think when you are in trance, and your conscious mind may well check in every so often to see if you're in trance and assure you that it is still there protecting and watching over you.

I know I said that it is impossible not to be able to wake up from a trance, but I did once have a subject on the stage who did not want to wake up at the end of the show. My suspicion was that her life was rather dull and being in a trance was a very nice place to be, not to mention the fact that she was getting a lot of attention from the audience and from me. So I got back into rapport with her, synchronizing my breathing and non-verbal behaviour, and once more asked her to wake up. She was still determined to stay in the trance that she was enjoying so much, so I simply turned to the person next to me and asked them to get me a bucket of cold water, making sure there was plenty of ice in it. She was awake two seconds later!

## ABREACTIONS

An abreaction is an unpleasant response that sometimes occurs in trance – a subject might burst into tears or shake. Such reactions usually result from the existence of painful memories stored at the unconscious level which being in a trance brings the subject into contact with. Within certain contexts this can be beneficial, and indeed many psychological therapies are based largely on getting a client to abreact.

Some therapists feel it is necessary to re-experience the pain of the past in order to release the emotional energy held in the unconscious. While there may indeed be some value in this, often what is really taking place is a recontextualizing, or a new evaluation, of the trauma from an older, wiser and safer perspective.

There are also those subjects who don't feel they have gained value from therapy unless they have a good cry. However, I firmly believe that handling the past does not have to be painful. Often in therapy clients do have to come to terms with suffering that has been denied in the past, but they don't have to go through it *all* again.

It is important to see an abreaction for what it is – a response to an experience – and dealing with it is straightforward. If subjects burst into tears, the hypnotist will get into rapport with them by pacing the experience, saying, 'You're crying and I don't know what exactly it is that you are feeling.' Then he or she could begin to lead the subject to a safe and healthy understanding of their experience. For example,

'As those tears run down your face, you can know that your unconscious mind knows that it is safe for you to experience this now. You don't have to make sense of it all here and now. Just know you can trust yourself to feel what you have to feel and then have a great sense of relief that you have been able to do so, and relish that sense of release and calm that comes after making a real step forward in healing the past.'

It's a mistake to assume that anyone who cries in trance necessarily feels bad; they may also shed tears after having an incredible insight.

Many people ask me to show them how to hypnotize others. I don't have a problem with that, but I do suggest that before they try to deal with other people's lives through hypnosis, they first get themselves sorted out. Hypnotic induction is straightforward and relatively safe, but using it properly is more complicated. Hypnosis enables you to play with the door to other people's realities and it's very important to be gentle when opening the door. Let me put it like this. Driving instructors can teach you how to drive, and how to drive well, but they can't tell you where to go. Learning the techniques of hypnosis is like learning to drive; using it well is like knowing where you want to go. If you are hypnotizing others, you are their chauffeur, so you have a responsibility to deliver them safely to the right destination.

## A SIMPLE INDUCTION EXPLAINED

What follows is a simple induction, with a parallel explanation of just some of the techniques and the language structure that are being used, which will give you a greater understanding of how a hypnotic induction works.

You are sitting here listening to me and wondering how it is you are going to **go into trance. Now,** I don't know if you will **go into trance quickly** or if you will take a little longer to **really enjoy** all the subtle **changes in your awareness** you notice as **it happens.**

We start with a truism, a pacing statement which tells the subject something they already know, linked to an indirect suggestion that presupposes the subject will go into trance. The words 'go into trance. Now' are **marked out** by a change in the tone of the hypnotist's voice. The questioning tone of the next sentence masks the embedded commands **go into trance quickly** and **really enjoy.** 'All the subtle **changes**' is a non-specific reference, allowing the hypnotist to hitch his or her further suggestions on whatever changes occur next in the subject's awareness. **it happens. Now** is also marked out.

**Now,** what I'd like you to do is just take a deep breath in and hold it, hold it, and let it go, and as you do, just let any tensions you had go as well, that's it, and you don't have to lose awareness of the weight of your body

Next the hypnotist asks the subject to change his or her breathing pattern, which will inevitably produce some subtle changes, which will begin to build evidence, and experience, of trance. By saying 'any tensions you had', the hypnotist puts the tensions in the past, and by remarking that 'you don't have to lose awareness' he or she introduces the possibility that the subject might just do so.

sitting here in the chair or your arms **resting** on your lap and your heavy eyelids blinking because they can just close your eyes, now only as fast as you begin going inside and

'sitting here' is another pacing statement, reinforcing rapport, and **resting**, marked out, is an indirect suggestion for rest. Talking next of blinking, a physiological inevitablility, added to 'heavy' and 'they can just close your eyes', makes the hypnotic response of eye closure seem impersonalized and hence automatic. Furthermore, the suggestion 'going inside', which introverts the attention, is made contingent on the inevitable eye closure of blinking.

**really relaxing**, and begin now counting backwards in your mind from 300, 299, 298, 297, 296, 295, 294, 293, back and back as you relax the little muscles at the side of your eyes, and your mouth, and those awarenesses spreading down through your throat and chest and stomach, as you become aware of that **increasing feeling of comfort** and relaxation spreading down through your legs and feet as it reaches the tips of your toes and your body can move if it wants as you **go deeper**, and from your shoulders, arms and the very tips of your fingers. . .

really relaxing is marked out, and then the conscious mind is offered an apparently simple, effortless but absorbing task to distract it and keep it occupied while the hypnotic suggestions are offered. A systematic relaxation of the body is started and all the words of comfort are marked out. At the same time, the hypnotist offers the possibility of dissociation from bodily experience even as it is rendered increasingly comfortable and passive by 'and your body can move if it wants as you' go deeper, inferring that the subject and his or her body are separate (with specific subjects in front of them, hypnotists would feed back the observed responses of their subjects).

I wonder if you've noticed yet, does one hand feel slightly heavier than the other hand, and one hand slightly warmer, sensing the weight of your hands as you go deeper, and

The innocent 'wonder' introduces another suggestion which is relatively easy for the subject to follow – our hands do normally feel in some way different. Drawing attention thoughts can be thought but you don't have to think them, you can notice words, notice noticing words, notice noticing, your body has relaxed, mind can relax to wander freely and pause because

to it amplifies our experience of this difference and allows it to become a focus of absorption of attention. 'thoughts can be thought' dissociates and depersonalizes processes we normally take as validation of our consciousness, and 'notice noticing words' overloads the conscious mind – it becomes easier and easier just to relax into trance and stop trying to do anything consciously.

when we go to the cinema we forget about the seat we are sitting in and really **become absorbed in the wonderful story**, and when you enjoy walking on a lovely summer's day, I don't know if you are more aware of the feeling of the ground beneath your feet or the warmth of the bright sunshine on your face and in the distance the enchanted castle looks so inviting as you make your way nearer and you find yourself here at the castle now opening the door revealing

'go to the cinema' is a metaphorical suggestion to become a passive observer and a stimulus for regression to a past experience. The following rich description appeals to all the senses, making the fantasy continually absorbing.

It leads into the scene that allows the unconscious mind to offer the suggestion most suitable for the client at this time. Note that the hypnotist here is not using the trance to implant his or her own ideas, but to open a channel of communication with the

the splendid entrance hall and the stairs that take you up to the first floor where you see a door, and behind that door is someone who has a special message for you, as the door creaks open and you step into what seems to be a beautiful big library, over there is someone smiling, it's your higher self and as you walk over and say hello, your higher self has a special message. Now I don't know if you will know that consciously now, or unconsciously [pause], that message that helps you in so many ways, even if you don't necessarily know exactly what they are yet, and as soon as you've thanked your higher self you make your way out of the library, down the stairs, leaving the castle in the distance

unconscious and allow the client's creativity to come up with a message that is exactly tailored to his or her own needs.

as you prepare to make your way back, confident in what you've learned, and as I count back from five to one you'll **awake refreshed, relaxed,**

The waking sequence is interspersed with positive suggestions which make coming out of trance both contingent upon, and a

**alert, feeling good,** bringing with you all the learning that you need and leaving those things that are best left at the unconscious level. Five, finding where your body is. Four, a nice stretch and yawn. Three, coming back. Two, you can really appreciate what an eye-opening experience trance is. One, you're wide awake.

validator of, the benefits of the trance.

# THE TEN STAGES OF TRANCE

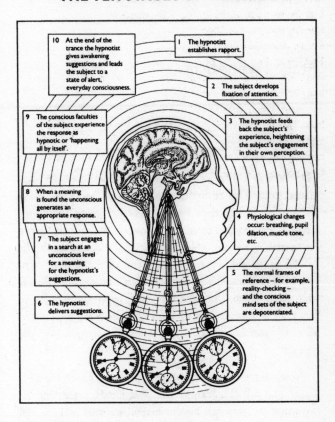

10 At the end of the trance the hypnotist gives awakening suggestions and leads the subject to a state of alert, everyday consciousness.

1 The hypnotist establishes rapport.

2 The subject develops fixation of attention.

9 The conscious faculties of the subject experience the response as hypnotic or 'happening all by itself'.

3 The hypnotist feeds back the subject's experience, heightening the subject's engagement in their own perception.

8 When a meaning is found the unconscious generates an appropriate response.

4 Physiological changes occur: breathing, pupil dilation, muscle tone, etc.

7 The subject engages in a search at an unconscious level for a meaning for the hypnotist's suggestions.

5 The normal frames of reference – for example, reality-checking – and the conscious mind sets of the subject are depotentiated.

6 The hypnotist delivers suggestions.

The subject can go through the stages over and over again and each element can be sustained while the next one is added. There are countless ways to go into trance, all variations great or small on this theme.

**4**

# Stage Hypnotism

## HISTORY

Hypnosis as a form of entertainment seems to have orig-
inated in the United States as long ago as the 1840s. Magnetism, as it was then known, was becoming incredibly
popular around that time and a group of individuals known
as 'missionaries' set about converting and educating the
public by giving demonstrations and exhibitions of hypnotic phenomena. These attracted large numbers of people
and from them the idea of stage hypnosis was born.
Looking at the content of these demonstrations as listed
in 1851, you can see that very little has changed over the
years.

Now tell him to open his eyes and put his hands together
. . . and say, 'You cannot get your hands apart', and he
cannot. . . Now tell him to extend his arm and . . . tell
him that he cannot put it down, and he cannot. If he is
well inducted, you may tell him that he cannot step, or
speak, or see, or hear, or taste, and he cannot. . . Tell him
that water is rum, or ink, or hot, or cold . . . that he is a

negro, a female, a dog, a fish, a post, a steam-engine – that his head is a coffee-mill – that he is Richard Hamlet, or what you please, and he is transformed instantly, and verily believes your assertion to be true.

From the exhibitions of these 'missionaries' came a new group of magnetic demonstrators calling themselves electrobiologists, who brought a touch of show business to the act of hypnosis. By the early 1850s records show that such performances were widespread across America, Canada and Europe, including Britain. Two particular performers seem to have attracted a lot of attention in Europe – Carl Hansen, a Dane, and one Donato, a Belgian.

These early showmen took the more spectacular hypnotic phenomena and made them entertaining. Accounts of Hansen's shows reveal that he had his subjects eating potatoes while thinking they were pears, drinking imaginary champagne and getting drunk, 'engaging in preposterous pantomines' and 'the striking of absurd attitudes'. Hansen toured widely and seems to have spawned a whole host of other stage hypnotists. He can be credited, along with other public performers, with increasing knowledge of the subject, and many of today's indicators of hypnotic susceptibility are recognizably similar to those used by Hansen when he entertained spectators more than a hundred years ago.

Exhibitions of stage hypnotism were top entertainments for some time, but unfortunately the art was steadily abused and for a while was reduced to a mockery of the real thing by fake hypnotists using stooges and crude routines that were often in very poor taste. Stage hypnosis then enjoyed a big revival at the beginning of this century with the success of an American hypnotist, Ormond McGill. His book on the subject, *The Encyclopedia of Genuine Stage Hypnotism*, advocates the performing of real stage hypnosis as opposed to trickery and contains some classic advice for anybody thinking of taking up the art – not to mention instructions on how to hypnotize a frog or a lobster, and how to use chloroform to anaesthetize the particularly stubborn subject!

Stage hypnosis in Britain enjoyed renewed success as a music hall act during the 1940s, when a hypnotist called Peter Casson played all the main venues and put hypnotism back on the theatrical map. In 1946 he caused a sensation in a feature for BBC television by inadvertently hypnotizing the engineers on the control panel while they were watching the broadcast.

In the 1950s an American hypnotist working in England, Ralph Slater was involved in a court case which filled the tabloids and is probably one of the chief factors responsible for stage hypnotism's bad reputation in this country. He lost his case in the lower court but did eventually win on appeal. However, by then the case had prompted efforts to get a bill through Parliament banning stage hypnotism completely. The first attempt was not successful, but a second, more moderate, duly became the Hypnotism Act (1952), which demands that all hypnotists performing stage hypnosis have a licence issued by the appropriate local licensing authority. It is, amusingly, only hypnotists and animal trainers who need such licences to perform. Essentially, the purpose of this act was public safety, and there is still a Home Office circular of recommended rules attached to every licence issued. These quite rightly protect the safety of the participants, as well as controlling shows that are known to be pornographic.

## 'PAUL McKENNA'S HYPNOTIC SHOW'

My own interest in hypnosis dates back to when I was nineteen and fascinated by Eastern religion, particularly Zen Buddhism. Books like Eric Berne's *Games People Play*, Alan Watts's *The Way of Zen* and Philip Kapleau's *Zen Dawn in the West* influenced me greatly at the time. Many religious practices involve trance-like states of meditation or the focusing of attention, so a lot of the groundwork was also laid by my interest in meditation, yoga, Za Zen, rebirthing and suchlike.

When I was working as the breakfast DJ on Chiltern Radio, a commercial station just outside London, I happened to interview a local hypnotist. As part of the piece I asked him to hypnotize me and was truly amazed at the experience, and particularly at the incredible sensory distortions it was possible to create, apparently with just words.

He lent me some books on the subject and when, a few weeks later, I happened to notice that a stage hypnotist was putting on a show at a theatre near me, I went along to watch. I had seen hypnotists before, but this time it all made sense. It was as though, about twenty minutes into the show, a light-bulb flashed on in my brain. All that I had read, all the theory, suddenly made sense and I could see exactly how hypnosis worked.

I started practising on friends and before long I was having, and creating, lots of fun at parties. Sometimes it worked and sometimes it didn't, but I was learning more all the time. Even now, with years of experience and countless shows under my belt, I'm still learning more and more about hypnosis.

I never misused the knowledge I acquired, but I certainly had a great time with it. One night when I was with some friends, one of them kept challenging me to hypnotize him, telling me that he couldn't be hypnotized and that there was no such thing as hypnosis anyway. I took up the challenge and spent about ten minutes talking to him, until he went out like a light. I put in post-hypnotic suggestions that he would not remember I had hypnotized him and every time anyone mentioned the trigger word 'Elvis' he would jump up and shout at the top of his voice, 'I believe in fairies.' Then we all went out to eat and for the rest of the evening – well, it was amazing how many times Elvis Presley's name came up in the conversation!

Nowadays I confine that sort of hypnotic fun to my stage show, but I did recently hear of a rather naughty misuse of hypnosis by a hypnotherapist who hypnotized his brother-in-law and left a post-hypnotic suggestion there allowing him to put his brother-in-law to sleep whenever he clicked his fingers, in the same way that a stage hypnotist does. A group of them would be playing cards and the hypnotherapist would lean over and click his fingers, putting his brother-in-law to sleep. The rest of them would then switch his cards around, instruct him to forget what had just taken place and wake him up, trying very hard to contain their laughter as he sat there wondering where his two aces had gone!

My original interest in hypnosis was, and to a large extent still is, as a tool for personal enhancement and self-discovery. However, it was while I was having fun with it that the performer in me saw the potential for a stage show. I started small and remember my very first show vividly. I persuaded a couple of friends who owned a pub near Cambridge to let me put on a performance there. The first week a handful of people turned up and I did my first show with a few sceptical volunteers. The following week I was as astonished as the landlords when about fifty curious people turned up to be hypnotized, and then completely bowled over when a week later the place was so full you couldn't get in the door. The whole village had turned out to see the goings-on at the local pub. There was only one thing for it: I went out, hired a theatre and 'Paul McKenna's Hypnotic Show' was born.

At that time, if you wanted to see a stage hypnotist you almost certainly had to travel to the end of a pier. The majority of them were middle-aged or elderly men sporting goatee beards, black shirts buttoned to the top and medallions around their necks. I went to a few of their shows and the main thing I noticed was that most of them humiliated their subjects to get laughs. While I think it is an integral part of the show to be cheeky, some stage hypnotists unfortunately make fools out of people.

When I was first starting out I went along to a lot of different shows. Although the routines the hypnotists used were often the same, the shows were always different. This is simply because every subject's imagination is completely different, and every show of mine is different for that reason. In my opinion stage hypnosis is a veritable gold-mine of comedy.

I decided right from the start to bring my show to a completely new public by performing only in theatres, thus avoiding the end-of-the-pier or night-club image that stage hypnosis seemed to have at the time. I felt that rather than laugh *at* people, audiences should be laughing *with* them. The beauty of stage hypnosis is the way a normally shy and quiet person can be completely transformed. They can stand confidently on a stage in front of two thousand people and become a comic genius! Normal inhibitions are bypassed through hypnosis and they access other previously undiscovered aspects of their imagination.

Many people would love to be performers but are prevented from realizing their dream by their natural fears of embarrassment or failure. They are held tightly in place by the confines of their everyday personas. While hypnotized on stage they can become Elvis Presley, Madonna or Michael Jackson and live out a fantasy. It's a kind of 3-D karaoke, and by this I don't mean that the participants are pretending or playing along. Some of them genuinely believe that they are these pop stars, while others simply carry out the suggestions without questioning why, because in hypnosis the conscious faculty is bypassed. It is a truly unique and wonderful state of fascination and absorption, and the great thing about coming along to one of my shows is that you can actually ask the participants just how it felt for them or volunteer yourself.

In 1988 I joined Capital Radio in London as a DJ and, although I was thrilled to be at such a prestigious radio station, confusingly enough there was still a part of me that was not completely fulfilled. However, Capital owned a theatre and promoted many of the big concerts in London, and as I was walking up the Tottenham Court Road one afternoon I suddenly realized that a truly great opportunity was staring me right in the face.

Coincidentally, one of my friends was experimenting with 'creative visualization' at the same time. The best way to describe this practice is to view the brain as a computer that is only as good as the programmes that run it; creative visualization is positive software for the brain. In the process of trying to help my friend improve his visualization techniques using hypnosis, I decided to try it out as well. In one visualization I asked my mind to take me into what it predicted would be my life five years in the future. I got quite a shock. I really hadn't progressed in career terms and spiritually, financially and emotionally I was worse off. So using some techniques we devised together, I began to create the kind of future I would like to have in my imagination and then I programmed it in. Later on I'll show you how to use some of these self-same techniques on yourself.

The first thing I noticed in doing this was the increase in my energy level. Suddenly, because I had a compelling future to look forward to, I was more enthusiastic and much more motivated. I firmly believe that you get back from life what you put out, so I started to put out more positive energy and I certainly began to get it back.

I approached the Programme Controller of Capital Radio, Richard Park, and asked him to help me promote my hypnotic show in the West End of London. He was delighted to agree. Next I went to my bank manager and asked for a loan (he wasn't sure at first, so I had to hypnotize him!). Then, filled with a mixture of excitement and fear, on a Sunday evening in December 1989 I stepped out on to the stage of the Duke of York's Theatre. Within two weeks the show was a sell-out, just as I had visualized a few months earlier.

It wasn't long before other performers, comedians and magicians came to check out my show, some concluding, 'It must be fixed.' It's understandable that if you're accustomed to highly organized performances, or an act that involves trickery and conventional sleight of hand, then it's difficult to appreciate one that is genuinely about members of the audience responding spontaneously to my suggestions. The most important thing was that the audiences enjoyed it, and came back time and time again. Whether it was to catch me out or figure me out, I didn't really mind.

My next break came after about six months when Harvey Goldsmith attended one evening with his brilliant right-hand man, Pete Wilson. I didn't know it at the time but this was to be a meeting that changed my life. Pete was fascinated by the show and decided to take it on immediately as his personal project. He was used to filling venues like Wembley Stadium with the likes of George Michael, U2 and Madonna and, to my initial concern, moved me to a venue five times the size of the one I had been playing. His judgement was spot-on, however, and the Dominion Theatre sold out all of its two thousand seats on the first night. The atmosphere in the theatre was electric. Playing a venue of that size adds something special to the show, and I still really enjoy performing there regularly.

I believe that word of mouth is the best form of advertising and for the show it certainly proved to be. The audiences grew as if by magic. Hypnosis is a word that carries a lot of suggestive baggage and therefore many preconceived ideas come to mind when it is mentioned, but my show seemed to tap into the positive, creative side of people's imaginations. The audiences seemed to understand the fun, the enjoyment and the creativity they could express straight away. At first we had to spend a lot of time convincing cynical journalists and producers that hypnosis was not evil, or dangerous, but now they mostly seem to pick the positive vibes up just by coming to the shows.

I remember a journalist from one of the Sunday papers at an after-show party telling a member of my staff that he was convinced it was all fixed and the participants were actors. When she offered to introduce him to me he jumped a mile and said no, because he was worried I would hypnotize him. Try and figure that one out!

An amusing problem we had in another venue relates to the 1952 Hypnotism Act, which, as I have said already, was brought in to protect the public from dangerous and pornographic hypnotists and is something I wholeheartedly support and promote. My show certainly follows the guidelines laid down by the Home Office and is, by those standards, safe and very much a family show.

When we want to play in a new area we have to apply for a licence from the local authority, and in most cases we have no problems with this. Unfortunately, there are still a small number of local authorities who have taken it upon themselves to protect their boroughs from 'the evils' of hypnotism, and indeed safeguard the morals and values of their residents, by banning *all* hypnotists. Recently, I was due to perform in Wimbledon but through a technicality in the licensing procedure the matter of the licence for my show came before a local council subcommittee. Two of the three councillors were very opposed to hypnotism and decided to use their position to ban my performance.

Obviously local councils do, and indeed should, have the power to prohibit performances of stage hypnotism if they constitute a danger to the public or if they are pornographic. They are not, however, supposed to act as censors, imposing their own personal tastes upon the public. I was shocked at their decision to ban me, and dreaded the thought of fifteen hundred annoyed people turning up at the theatre in two days' time.

Other members of the council and the licensing officers helped me get the matter into the magistrates' court the very next day. When I turned up there, I couldn't help thinking that the lawyer representing me looked familiar. Incredibly, it turned out that I had actually hypnotized him on stage a few months earlier, so he understood my show very well.

The 'trial' was almost as entertaining as one of my shows.

I took the stand and was asked a number of questions about the nature of the show and actually had to demonstrate what a Chippendale or Madonna does on stage to decide if it was 'lewd and sexual'. The best part came when the two councillors opposing the show took the stand and unintentionally became our best witnesses:

LAWYER: Why did you decide to ban Paul McKenna?

COUNCILLOR: I don't approve of stage hypnosis.

LAYWER: Why not?

COUNCILLOR: It's humiliating and degrading.

LAWYER: Have you ever seen 'Paul McKenna's Hypnotic Show'?

COUNCILLOR: No.

LAWYER: I see. Have you seen any stage hypnotist?

COUNCILLOR: No.

LAWYER: Then how can you say it's humiliating?

COUNCILLOR: I just think it is.

LAWYER: I've seen Mr McKenna's show, and indeed I've taken part in it, and I didn't feel humiliated. How do you explain that?

COUNCILLOR: Well, that's your opinion.

LAWYER: Thank you. No more questions.

We won the case and our costs, and the show was a huge success. The one factor both the Press and the council cannot ignore is that venues normally reserved for rock concerts are packed to see a hypnotist night after night. At the end of the day, as long as the audience and the participants are coming back again and again, I know I am doing something right.

So, the stage show continued to grow and took a leap forward when television producer Paul Smith, the man responsible for 'It'll Be All Right on the Night' (among many other innovative shows), approached me about making a light-entertainment series of my stage show for Carlton Television. I'm delighted to have this opportunity to bring hypnosis to a wider public. It looks as though this first series will lead on to further projects. Although it is an entertainment show, considering the broader picture, I hope also that this demonstration of the amazing powers of the human mind will lead more people to use hypnosis to improve their day-to-day life and health.

The other thing I can thank my stage shows for is a chance meeting with somebody I might otherwise not have got to know. It was at a show at Guildford Civil Hall, and when I first began hypnotizing the volunteers I noticed something strange about one of the subjects, a girl with striking long blonde hair. As she began to perform the routines, however, her hair began to move about and I, as well as the audience, realized that she was wearing a wig. A million thoughts raced through my mind: should I take it off – perhaps she had no hair – and why was she wearing a wig in the first place?

Eventually I asked her to nip off the stage, where my stage manager took the wig off her, revealing . . . long blonde hair. She came back on stage but I couldn't stop wondering about her and her hair! After the show, at the side of the stage, I gave her the wig back and she explained that she had come with a friend of hers who was a celebrity and hadn't wanted to be recognized being hypnotized, so they had both worn wigs as a prank.

I was dying to get to know her better, as they say, but knew it would be unprofessional and perhaps even unethical to ask to see her again under these circumstances. So we said goodbye and I thought that was that, until a few days later a friend of mine rang up and told me that he knew 'the girl in the wig'. He fixed up dinner, invited Clare along and the rest is history. Although Clare is a writer, she finds time to work alongside me, organizing the many aspects of my shows, doing the stage management and handling the Press, as well as helping me coordinate my schedule.

Another lucky break came when I met my agent at International Creative Management (ICM), Dennis Sellinger. Dennis is Britain's most powerful and successful entertainment agent and has been a great help to me, due to the enormous respect in which he is held by people in the industry.

In the two years I played the Dominion Theatre, I never took for granted that I would manage to fill the venue again and again, and so it came as a huge surprise when Pete Wilson told me that I was to play the Royal Albert Hall in only three weeks' time. I thought it would be impossible to fill such a place in such a short amount of time, but we sold it out. I have to say that when I walked on to that famous stage on 1 December 1992, I felt wonderful – very lucky and very privileged – and I earned a place in the record books for the biggest show of stage hypnosis in the world!

I get more questions about my show than about any other aspect of my work, and people often ask what is the funniest thing that has ever happened, or if anything has ever gone wrong, or if I have ever had nobody volunteer and so on. Well, I have been performing my stage show for nearly six years now, and sometimes I think I have seen it all – until somebody does something, or says something, that makes me laugh just as much as a member of the audience seeing the show for the first time.

Recently I asked one of the subjects what it felt like when he was in trance and, without hesitating, he replied, 'Toffee Angel Delight'. I think that is as good as, if not better than, any description I could come up with. It is, however, during the routine 'The World's Greatest Liars' that I think the most incredible examples of comic genius appear. At this point of the show I tap straight into the unconscious mind of the subject and get an incredible glimpse into the unlimited potential of the human imagination.

I have had a Concorde pilot complaining about the air traffic police fining them for speeding; footballers explaining in great detail about the new rules of the game, such as how the managers are now in goal and get two salaries as a result; Sarah Ferguson denying it was her body in *those* photos and saying they had superimposed Diana's body on her head; Nigel Mansell boasting about how he had raced Ayrton Senna; the Queen and a Jack Russell on the way to the theatre; and a man introducing himself as Watchtower Number Five in 'Baywatch'. One lady claimed she was Lord Nelson but had also been Rasputin, Pythagoras and Enid Blyton; another man said he was

Crispin Tightpenny, a fraud officer who had uncovered Robert Maxwell's money in Waddington's Monopoly boxes – he was a cross-dresser and usually walked his beat in deck shoes but that night was wearing high heels and tripped as a result. The speed at which these subjects access such obscure and bizarre information is quite incredible and, as a result, this is the section of the show I particularly look forward to.

The interval routines, however, when I send people out into the theatre audience, each with their own specific persona, also makes for some hilarious results. Recently I sent one man out thinking he was a guru who would come out with wise words. I asked him to give us an example of his wisdom and he came out with, 'A man with a fiddle can play with himself' and 'You can lead a horse to water but you can't get those little pieces of sweetcorn out from between your teeth.' Now that's wisdom for you!

I consider stage hypnotism as much an art as anything else. Even though there are a few therapists who deride the use of hypnosis 'merely' for entertainment, others have acknowledged that its great benefit is it shows people *hypnosis works*.

I am frequently asked by people who see my stage show how exactly I do it. It is difficult for me to reply with an honest one-sentence answer – in the future I will just respond by telling those people to read my book! So let's look more closely at the structure of the show.

## BEHIND THE SCENES

### Stage-Show Techniques

Let me take you behind the scenes. I am frequently asked about the technical aspects of my show by people who come and enjoy it. Of course, the first thing they want to know about is how I set up the induction.

### The Suggestibility Test

Most stage hypnotists use some sort of suggestibility test or exercise as a way of gauging their subjects. It is not essential but over the years I have found it helpful in many ways. First, it helps the audience and participants to get to know me as much as it helps me to spot the more instantly imaginative subjects.

Usually I ask people to clasp their hands together, imagining that the hold is getting tighter and tighter. Rather than looking for those with their hands stuck together, I am more concerned with how people approach the exercise. I am looking for immediate psychological responses; body language plays an important part in my selection process.

The 'forward-sway test' is another technique. Here subjects are asked to put their feet together and arms by their sides and stand approximately two feet from the hypnotist, while looking into his or her eyes, and then let themselves fall forwards. This has many functions, including showing pretty quickly who is prepared to let themselves go. Also, while falling forwards, they concentrate upon the hypnotist's face, thereby associating him or her with an experience of letting go.

## Inductions

Visually I make my first inductions rapid, asking subjects to fall forwards or backwards (see photograph). This is dramatic – remember, stage hypnotism is show business! It demonstrates just how quickly hypnosis can happen, and it also gives me more room on the stage!

The next subjects are induced by progressive relaxation. I think it is important to show the full hypnotic process, because it is undoubtedly fascinating, as well as adding credibility and authenticity. When I first started with stage shows, once I did a rapid induction on all the subjects together. Following my selection, I just turned to the subjects and simply told them to sleep. I was happy about how slick it looked and the time it saved, but some members of the audience found it difficult to believe that I could hypnotize people so rapidly.

As I begin giving suggestions, I watch to see how the various subjects are responding. Some people go into trance and, while they enjoy it and follow my instructions, are not that visually animated. I find the best subjects for stage hypnosis are lively and uninhibited, even though this may not be their everyday persona.

I make my selection of those subjects I intend to use for the rest of the evening while doing some simple 'run-up' routines. First, getting them to imagine they are simple things like goldfish, Miss World or a washing machine, and then going into bigger routines like riding a horse, or whatever they do at 3.30 on a Monday afternoon. I install safety suggestions so that all the subjects are protected by their unconscious minds. As the show gets under way the imaginative capabilities of the participants are being explored as I ask them, say, to become a naughty class of five-year-old children, Martians, pop stars, a sergeant-major, a champion footballer, the world's greatest liar . . . to mention some of the routines that are popular at the moment.

At the end of the show all the hypnotic suggestions are removed and I always ask the audience to acknowledge the subjects as the stars of the show. I never know what is going to happen as I walk out on to the stage at the beginning of the evening, but I guess that is what makes it constantly exciting and challenging for me.

# 5

# Hypnotherapy

## THE DIFFERENT APPROACHES

We all have our own immune system. The body and mind work together to regulate, protect and heal the fantastic vessel that we essentially are. We live in an age when incredible medical advances are taking place all the time. Drugs and techniques of surgery have become much more reliable. Many people expect instant cures for their ills and hand over responsibility for their health to the medical profession, preferring a prescription to instigating a change in their lifestyle or diet.

The cultural acceleration of prescription drugs has led to other problems. Some reports suggest that more people are killed each year by prescribed drugs in the USA and Britain than are killed in road accidents.

Our immune system is partially a function of the unconscious, and through hypnosis the healing process can be accelerated. Research has shown that many people who believed they could control their immune system, in fact did so using hypnotic techniques. These individuals could actually increase the number of protective blood cells in their bodies, thus improving their resistance to illness. We are only just beginning to understand the incredible power of hypnosis and its potential role in the medicine and therapy of the future.

If you are thinking of trying hypnotherapy, then broadly speaking it falls into two categories: direct and indirect.

## Direct Hypnotherapy

Practitioners of direct hypnotherapy are often authoritarian in approach (rather similar, in fact, to a stage hypnotist), telling the subject what to do. Some authoritarian or command therapists adopt a superior attitude. They assume the role of expert, with the client there to be told what to do, taking the role of a passive receiver for the therapist's suggestions.

The problem with this approach is that if the client is unable to accept the therapist's suggestions or analysis of the problem, then the therapy is ineffective. The relationship is very one-sided and doesn't use the client's own personal inner resources. In this sort of environment there is a subtle pressure on the client to accept the therapist's analaysis like 'a good client should'. If he or she is unable to do this, then the client may be called 'wrong' or labelled resistant or even unhypnotizable.

Finally, the authoritarian therapist tends to have fixed ways of approaching a case, rather than treating each one individually. This usually results in therapists installing their own model of happiness within the client, whether it is appropriate or not. As American therapist and writer

Leslie Cameron Bandler has said, 'Too many people leave therapy cured of their therapists' problems.'

*Indirect Hypnotherapy*

Practitioners of indirect hypnotherapy bypass any conscious resistance from the client to their suggestions. People are not viewed as broken but as having all the inner resources (even if only at an embryonic level) already within themselves. Indirect hypnotherapy, rather than focusing upon the aura of the hypnotist, emphasizes the relationship between therapist and client.

The perfect example of an indirect hypnotherapist was Milton Erickson. In his view there was no such thing as a resistant client, but only inflexible therapists.

Rather than pressurizing the client to accept their suggestions, indirect hypnotherapists create new ways of looking at a situation or coming up with more choices about behaving in the world. Often indirect hypnotherapists will help the new alternatives develop from within the client rather than installing them from the outside.

I think that either method can be used, and it is the skill of the hypnotist that decides which is appropriate. I use the authoritarian style on stage and tend to follow a more indirect style for therapy. The only time I find the need to use a direct approach is if the client wants or expects a direct command: to make them stop smoking, for example. In that situation, I perform most of the work indirectly but at the end will say directly in a forceful way that they will stop smoking. On occasions I do the work covertly with a client while they are in the waking state, then put them through a formal trance which essentially just reinforces the work that has already been done. On some occasions I do therapeutic work with people I meet during what seems like a simple conversation. I might just suggest that we all have the ability to ask someone to look at a problem in a different way. As I have said, the more flexible the therapists, the more positive the outcomes they can produce.

## TECHNIQUES

There are many different techniques in hypnotherapy. I have outlined the principal ones, with their individual pros and cons, to give you an overall understanding.

### Direct Suggestion

This is the old-fashioned, traditional technique. Once the trance has been induced and the hypnotist has direct access to the client's unconscious mind, he or she offers instructions to create the desired changes, saying something like, 'You will stop smoking.'

However, if the suggestion conflicts with the client's values, it will not be accepted. At best the client may stop smoking temporarily, but they will soon start again. When Coué pioneered suggestion, he realized this and found that a suggestion can be ingrained through sheer repetition. However, if a suggestion is not accepted, there is probably a very good reason, so the therapist should find out why, or choose another, more suitable suggestion.

There is often what is called a 'secondary gain' from addictive or repeated behaviour. Some people find it difficult to understand why anyone smokes cigarettes: it looks like a dirty, socially unacceptable habit, and is expensive and bad for your health. However, the secondary gain for smokers is that through cigarettes they control how they feel. Emotionally every day has its ups and downs, some of the changes minor and some dramatic. Smokers can control the intensity of the experience with a cigarette. It's like having a literal smokescreen between yourself and life.

That is why many smokers are habitual in their smoking, having a cigarette regularly at the telephone, after sex or a meal. There is an obvious risk in taking away this emotional support system with a direct suggestion like, 'You will stop smoking.' If clients don't have the flexibility to create new ways of handling their emotions, they will have to revert to cigarettes.

*Hypnoanalysis*

This is a form of psychoanalysis in the context of trance and is based on the work of Sigmund Freud and Carl Jung. They believed that present problems were the result of traumas from the past, often from childhood. These traumas may be forgotten or repressed, but the emotional scars still influence behaviour in the present. It has been said that if you continually look for something you will surely find it, so if you are always searching for reasons why you are 'messed up', then you will most likely find some.

Psychoanalysis has its place, and can lead to great rewards in terms of personal development – if you have the time and the money. However, I frequently meet people who have been in therapy for years and are pursuing complete under-standing of the cause of their problem through psycho-analysis. Unfortunately, they are taking a long time to get there, and rather wish that their immediate problems could be cured right now. Sometimes, in fact, we meet people who do know what went wrong, and with whom, when and how, yet they still feel terrible. Strategic hypnotherapy can help people begin to improve their life by starting with the events of the present. Many people are carrying pain in the present and do need to confront it and deal with it, but they don't have to dredge up every piece of pain they have ever felt and experience it all over again. I find that when people begin to change and deal with the challenges, and perhaps the pain, that face them in the present, they begin to understand the past in a different and healthier way.

In his book *Unlimited Power* Anthony Robbins uses the analogy of a jukebox in describing neurological activity. He says:

The human being keeps having experiences that are being recorded. We store them in the brain like records in a jukebox. As with the records in a jukebox, our recordings can be played back at any time if the right stimulus in our environment is triggered, if the right button is pushed.

The practice of psychoanalysis is well intentioned, but it was developed at a time when psychology was in its infancy. Nowadays there are more effective and less painful ways of achieving the same results by 'reprogramming the jukebox' so that it plays happy memories instead of sad ones.

As Richard Bandler states in *Using Your Brain for a Change*, when he looked into the field of psychology all he could find were 'descriptions of how people were broken'. He goes on: 'The current Diagnostic and Statistical Manual III used by psychiatrists and psychologists has over 450 pages of descriptions of how people can be broken, but not a single page describing health.'

## Age Regression

This approach does go into somebody's past to uncover traumas, but in a way that ultimately empowers the person by giving them a new way of looking at the situation. This is why regression is such an important technique in hypno-therapy. With all of our life's experiences recorded and stored in multi-sensory memories, we can go back and review any of them in a way that offers new and beneficial insights.

I am happy to believe that traumatic events which have shaped our behaviour are often kept at an unconscious level and that, using hypnosis through age regression, a client can go back to an incident of trauma and review a decision that might have been made early in life in a moment of intense emotion from the new, adult point of view.

## Future Progression

This is another way for an individual to see things from a new perspective. A problem becomes recontextualized when someone looks back at their life from the future and sees it in a larger frame. Future progression is also used to go to an imagined future in which an individual has certain skills which can gradually be brought back to the present and learned in a fraction of the time it would normally take.

## Parts Therapy

This comes from the work of Virginia Satir and Gestalt therapy. It presupposes that we have many parts to ourselves, based on the way that humans organize themselves. People actually say there's a part of them that wants to do something and a part that doesn't. The hypnotist will essentially talk with the part that is causing a problem for the client and negotiate an agreeable settlement to the situation between all the different parts of the same person.

## Visualization or Mental Rehearsal

These are used to enhance physical and mental changes and well-being. Because the nervous system cannot distinguish between reality or a vividly imagined experience, a sensory-rich experience of a desired new behaviour can be created during trance and encoded into the client's unconscious mind. For example, clients with a fear of public speaking can rehearse speaking in their imagination to a group of people successfully so that when they come to do it for real they will have 'past successes' to draw upon and feel good about.

Some therapists use visualization techniques in the treatment of diseases, asking clients to imagine healing taking place in particular parts of the body. A technique that I have found very successful with my clients in helping to accelerate the healing process is to get them to imagine breathing in a healing blue aura, a blue light shining brighter in the area where it is needed. I also suggest that the uncomfortable sensations can be breathed out with each breath.

These are some of the most popular and effective approaches a hypnotherapist might use. There are, of course, many variations and further possibilities. The best therapist will tailor every intervention to the needs of each particular client. It is important, however, to remember that with hypnotherapy a client must want to get better or change and accept the challenges of a life free of their limiting complaint. They must be prepared to forgo their 'secondary gain'. Hypnotherapy is very much a co-operative process, and so the therapist and client must be prepared to investigate and work with the *motivation for change* as well as the change itself.

If you are interested in training to become a hypnotherapist, see page 232.

## SPORTS HYPNOSIS

In Shakespeare's words, 'Our doubts are traitors,/And make us lose the good we oft might win,/By fearing to attempt' (*Macbeth*).

Over the years I have worked with many sports people, including Britain's top swimmer and Olympic Gold medalist Adrian Moorhouse and British fencer Johnny Davis, helping them to harness the power within themselves to improve their sporting performances.

Sports psychology has been around for quite a few years. As long ago as the 1950s the Soviet Olympic teams were using hypnotists to enhance athletic performance, and today it is a rapidly expanding area of interest all around the world.

Hypnosis can literally make you stronger and it has been proved that mental attitude has an incredible effect even on our physical powers. J. A. Hadfield, a famous British psychiatrist, gives a striking illustration of this in his book *The Psychology of Power*. He tested three men's strength by having them grip a dynamometer under three different sets of conditions. First, under normal waking consciousness their average grip was measured and it was 101 lb. The men were then hypnotized and told that they were very weak. When their grip was measured, it was just 29 lb (less than a third of their normal strength). Last of all, they were told under hypnosis that they were very strong. They were then able to grip 142 lb. When their minds were filled with positive thoughts of strength, they increased their actual physical powers by almost 50 per cent.[1]

A large part of achievement in sport is believing you can do it – it works like a self-fulfilling prophecy. Remember the saying, 'Whether you say you can or say you can't you are right.' A good example of this is the four-minute mile. For centuries humans have tried to run faster; the ancient Greeks even pulled men along with horses to improve their speed. In more recent times a cultural belief developed that it was impossible to run fast enough to break the four-minute mile, but in 1956 Roger Bannister 'did the impossible'. What is really incredible is the number of people who did the same soon after he did. Today hundreds of people have achieved it – not just because everybody suddenly became fitter, but because they believed it was possible.

In his book *The Inner Game of Tennis*, W. Gallwey suggests that the real opponent is not the other player on the tennis court but the opponent in our head: the negative internal representations, the nagging critical voice, or pictures of losing rather than representations of encouragement.

Most sports psychologists favour mental rehearsal, imagining the game, race or event going as the competitor wishes, over and over in their imagination. This sends a message from the mind to the body and fixes it in the body's kinaesthetic intelligence through repetition. However, this process on its own may not be effective. Not only *what* you represent internally but also *how* you represent it matters. I once worked with an athlete who had done hours of mental rehearsal and had seen himself winning over and over again. However, the pictures he made of himself were very small and dull, and when I asked him to think of his competitors, the pictures were big and bright. Everyone's representations are unique but, generally speaking, positive images are seen in a big, bright way. The way we represent something – brightness and the size – is the coding our brain uses to understand it. So I simply asked him to make a picture of himself bigger and brighter than that of his competitors. Location can be important too, and, sure enough, all his competitors were higher up, which for him meant they were better. We changed that round as well.

I worked with another athelete who represented all his competitors as larger than himself and bright with glowing suntans. I simply got him to swap the images round so that he now was larger and had the suntan. Immediately his behaviour changed – he no longer felt frightened and went out and won. Of course, it is not always as simple as that, and sometimes I have to hunt around for hours to get an understanding of how someone is mapping their world so that I can get them to make the appropriate change.

At the end of the day, it is the sports people themselves and only them who can win. All the sports psychologist can do is help that process, the way any coach does. However, there are many approaches available these days. When I was working with Johnny Davis, I would get him to step out of his body and into his opponent's, and then he would fence against himself, all the time noticing his opponent's body posture and strategies and his own. When Johnny came to fight, he suddenly found himself automatically manoeuvring in ways he had never tried before, because his unconscious had been able to incorporate some of the skills of his greatest opponents and experience his own style from a new perspective.

This is an incredibly effective technique for all sports people, amateur or professional. Here it is, step by step:

1    Watch a number of good performances of a role model or personal hero.

2    Relax into trance (sitting or standing).

3    Imagine a representation in front of you of your idealized image or role model engaged in whatever activities you admire most about him or her. Build up the image as richly and strongly as possible; see as much detail as you can, adding sounds and feelings.

4    In your imagination, ask your role model for help and notice his or her willingness to oblige.

5    Walk up behind your role model and step inside his or her body. Put him or her on like a suit. See with his or her eyes, hear with his or her ears and feel what he or she feels. (If you are standing when you take a step forward in your imagination, take a step forward physically.)

6    Explore what it is like to be in the world of your role model. If you have any questions about how he or she does something, find the answers while in his or her body.

7    When you have finished, step back out of your role model. Thank him or her for the help and return to

normal waking consciousness, bringing with you what you have learned. Remember, you have learned more than you are consciously aware of.

If yours is a sport that involves an opponent, then play yourself and find out your strengths and weaknesses. Incidentally, you don't have to limit this technique to sport; you can step into anyone who displays some skill you wish to acquire, or you can use the approach to see something from someone else's point of view. Try stepping into your boss's shoes.

## STRESS CONTROL

Although stress is a concept commonly referred to these days, it used to be thought of as something that affected only a few managers and executives in highly pressured jobs. The truth is that it affects nearly all of us.

We all need a certain amount of stress to motivate us to do things like get out of the way of oncoming cars. This could be called positive stress. However, continual inappropriate arousal of our mind and body can lead to illnesses. This is most definitely negative stress and is what I will be talking about in the following section.

The stress response is innate: our ancestors needed extreme physical reactions and bursts of energy to enable them to fight wild animals or run away. For example, when the mind perceives a threat, the heartbeat quickens, automatically the pupils dilate, muscles tighten, adrenalin is released into the bloodstream, the digestive process halts, blood pressure rises and the immune system is suppressed. This is the fight-or-flight response. If you are about to be attacked, then you need energy to respond to the situation. The problem, however, is that we are continually preparing for emergencies that never happen. This puts a strain on us.

These days we do not have to be constantly on the lookout for wild animals, but the twentieth century is full of threats from all kinds of different sources. Many people are always responding to what I call the power of negative thinking. They wake up in the morning and think to themselves, 'I must get up or I'll be in trouble.' Of course they don't want to be in trouble, because they might get fired and then they would not be able to pay the mortgage and would end up on the streets, etc. Even though they may not consciously have this exact chain of thoughts, it is there as a subtle backdrop.

This effectively is a constant attempt to avoid pain rather than go for pleasure. A positive approach is to wake up and think of all the things you are looking forward to doing that day; ask yourself what you would look forward to if you could.

Any average 'day in the life' has its demands and stresses – driving to work you get stuck in a traffic jam; you have an argument; you receive an unexpected bill; the kids have made a mess; you are criticized. These things may not seem like threats to you, but your nervous system does not differentiate between a physical threat to yourself and a threat to your ego. The stress response is being unnecessarily aroused all day long. These stresses may sometimes go unnoticed but they are there in bad moods, depression, mistakes and even physical problems. It is often only when we relax that we notice the tension that was there all the time.

Many times when you feel bad it is a product of your own stress response. That is why in our culture some people turn to alcohol, cigarettes or drugs to change the way they feel – to cope with stress. As continual negative stress can lead to diseases, this is a problem that needs to be dealt with.

Recent research has shown that the mind and body have their own patterns of rest or alertness, with one predominant cycle that occurs approximately every ninety minutes. This is when the body stops externally oriented behaviour and takes about fifteen minutes to relax and replenish its energy. This has become known as the ultradian rhythm – those moments in which you find yourself day-dreaming, when a gentle feeling is present in your body. It is quite simply the body's own natural stress-control system.

Unfortunately, many people override the message from their body that it is time to relax a little, and instead they have another cup of coffee or try even harder to concentrate. After a while they establish a pattern of overriding the ultradian rhythm. I believe that the major threat in modern life is being killed by our own defence system, because it has been triggered too often.

## Controlling Stress

Stress control is one of the things that I am often employed to deal with in the corporate world. Here are some simple techniques that everyone can use to diminish stress. You don't have to work for a corporation to benefit from them!

A simple and highly effective way to begin handling stress is to use the natural system we all possess in the ultradian rhythm. In future, whenever you find yourself day-dreaming and a feeling of comfort starting in your body, go with it and allow yourself to really relax for ten or fifteen minutes. You will return to your chores feeling refreshed and with better concentration afterwards.

The first researcher of physiological consequences of stress, Hans Selye, felt that, 'The most important stresses for man are emotional.' He went on to say, 'It is not the event but rather our intepretation of it that causes our emotional reaction.'

By interpreting our experiences differently we can begin to respond more to the events in our life rather than just reacting. You can refer to the sections on 'Framing' (pages 40–47) and Chapter Six for ways of looking at things differently.

Practising self-hypnosis is a good way of giving your mind and body a deep way of relaxing. I often relax into trance and imagine myself sunbathing on an exotic beach. Given, as I have said, that the nervous system does not differentiate between a real and a vividly imagined event, when I awake from a trance like that I feel as though I have just been on holiday – and, as far as my nervous system is concerned, I have.

Finally, it is also worth mentioning that aerobic exercise is important in controlling stress. Swimming, running or any exercise that oxygenates the blood makes controlling stress easier.

## HYPNOTIC TAPES

My main reason for looking at the tape market was that I was being inundated with requests to help people stop smoking, lose weight, control stress and so on, but I just didn't have the time to help every single person. There is an ever increasing number of hypnotic or self-help tapes on the market these days, both video and audio. Many of them are American and, as you would expect, some are very good, some very poor and the rest are somewhere in the middle.

So, fuelled by the desire to make something unique that I knew could help a lot of people. I set about creating a range of self-help hypnotherapy videos. One of my initial motivations was the absolute lack of good-quality video and audio tapes. Most are beautifully packaged but the quality of the hypnotic work inside is poor, and in some cases could even leave the customer worse off than they were when they started. One man has recorded over a hundred titles. This looks very impressive on the shelves until you realize all he is done is call the same subject by five different names. Another video series features an authoritarian hypnotist adopting a threatening tone to get you to relax completely!

Once I had decided to make my own range of videos, I gathered a team of specialists to work on the project with me, including a brilliant therapist who is an Ericksonian hypnotist with his own private practice. We worked together for months, crafting the first four tapes: *Stop Smoking Now!*, *Successful Slimming*, *Control Stress* and *Better Sex for Lovers*.

The format of these four tapes is similar. The first ten minutes are an introduction, giving practical advice and context setting. Next come two twenty-minute trances, featuring beautiful natural imagery mixed with Ericksonian hypnotic language. The effect upon the viewer can be profound. Many hardened forty-to-sixty-a-day smokers have stopped; some people have lost several stone in weight in just a few months; and people with stress and blood-pressure problems are back to normal, much to the surprise of their GPs. The next four titles, *Supreme Self-Confidence*, *Positive Thinking*, *Sleep Like a Log* and *Energy for Everyday*, are already proving as popular.

If you could bottle hypnosis, it would undoubtedly be the most powerful drug in the world, but you can't! However, you can put it on to tape, which is just as good. In the same way that some drugs are better than others, some hypnotic tapes are better than others.

### 'Lifeworks'

Although I had made my set of video tapes for retail sale, I also made many other audio tapes for myself and friends, and had incredibly positive results. I wanted to put the real power of these assorted tapes into one set, so I teamed up with my colleague Michael Breen and the result of our work together is a tape series called 'Lifeworks'. I am personally very proud of these tapes, because not only were they recorded using digital 24-track state-of-the-art technology but they also incorporate the latest in mind-body linguistics.

'Lifeworks' are designed so that you don't consciously have to understand everything that is said by Michael and me. You simply sit back and listen, then over the next few days and weeks begin to enjoy the wonderful changes you experience in yourself and your life.

You can obtain my tapes directly from me if you wish by writing to:

Paul McKenna
PO Box 4RS
London W I A 4RS

You can also write to this address if you want to be put on Paul McKenna's mailing list. Please send a s.a.e.

# 6

# You are under State Control

## WHAT STATE ARE YOU IN?

Have you ever witnessed exactly the same event as someone
else and yet found out later that you both have completely
different accounts of it? You were in the same place at the
same time, so how come you perceived it so differently?
The answer is, it all depends on the neurophysiological
state you were both in. Quite simply, love, anger, confidence, fear, apathy, happiness, fascination and so on are all
states of being, and we are constantly going in and out of
these different states all day long. Each of them is individual and unique to us. A state can be defined as the
sum total of all the neurological process occurring within
somebody at any one time which defines the mood they are
in. The majority of our states are not formed consciously
but unconsciously. Something happens to us and we react
to it by changing state automatically.

Different stimuli are constantly entering our environment and we receive information about them through our
five senses. That information is then filtered down by the
unconscious mind to the messages that reach our conscious

mind in the form of the pictures we make in our heads and the little voice that is constantly chattering away all day long. These internal images and sounds are referred to as *internal representations*, and they are only that – representations of reality and not what actually happened. Your representations are unique to you; they are your own personal way of perceiving the world.

So why do we represent reality to ourselves? It is because the conscious mind can process only a handful of ideas at any one time, although the unconscious mind processes two million messages of sensory awareness every single second. It would simply be overwhelming to sort reality consciously, trying to work out every one of the millions of sensations bombarding our awareness every second of the day. For that reason we filter reality, and as our filters are created from our values, beliefs and focus of interest from moment to moment, we constantly sort reality to find what we believe is important and useful to us. It is this filtering process that explains the difference in people's perceptions, because everyone's filter is different.

An excellent way of seeing our filter is as a map. We experience life through our own map of the world, because a map is only a representation – or, in other words, *the map is not the territory*. The world is infinitely richer than the way we think of it, and the kind of maps we make of it create the kind of world we live in. If our map of the world is one of happiness and excitement, our life will reflect that. If it is one based on the belief that life is boring, mundane and harsh, then it will reflect that. Like one big self-fulfilling prophecy, your map is your focus in life, and the golden rule is, as always: You always get more of what you focus on. It's not what happens to you in life but how you choose to represent it to yourself. Everything that I am saying in this book is shaped by my personal filter of hypnosis and reality, and the ideas that fit your map will undoubtedly be more useful to you than those that don't.

Although human beings are truly fascinating in their individuality, at one level they are really like stimulus-response machines, and rather robotic in their understanding of right and wrong. For example, for some people dancing is a very good activity, because it puts them in a state of excitement, but to others dancing is a very bad activity, interpreted as an act of exhibitionism, and puts them in a state of self-consciousness. There is no fixed meaning attached to any state in life except the meaning we create.

If you think about it, the things you constantly *say* to yourself internally have an incredibly profound impact. Most of the time you are judging and evaluating, and use different tones of voice to put you in a particular state. For example, consider the tone of voice you use to criticize yourself. Who does it sound like? Your teachers? Your parents? What tone of voice is it? What do you say to yourself when you make a mistake? Is it, 'Oh, good. Another learning experience.' I doubt it. It's probably something more like, 'You really screwed up this time' or, 'When are you ever going to learn?' One of my clients said to me that if he talked to other people the way he talked to himself, he'd be arrested! Of course we all say nice things to ourselves too. Ask yourself, what kind of voice do I use for that? Maybe you could use that voice a little more often. . .

There are other ways to change a critical voice too. You can speed it up so it sounds like Mickey Mouse, or slow it down and change the tone of it so it sounds sexy and less threatening.

Furthermore, everybody has the ability to visualize. If you are suffering from the delusion that you cannot, simply think of your front door and what colour it is. In order to do this you have to go into your imagination and make a picture of it. Do it now. Notice if your picture is in colour or black and white, dim or bright, and where it's located – is to the right of you, to the left or directly in front of you?

As well as *what* we represent, it is *how* we represent things in our heads that determines our state from moment to moment. If you picture a time when you felt really bad, it changes your state, likewise, if you think of a time when you felt ecstatic, on top of the world, that changes your state as well. In order to think of something you have to go inside and give yourself a little bit of that feeling.

The power of the pictures we make in our head is the basis of creative and positive visualization techniques. These pictures are incredibly powerful. Right now, if you say to your heart 'Beat faster', it won't make any difference, but if you imagine walking down a sinister, dark alley late at night, your heartbeat will speed up. This demonstrates the powerful link between the mind and the body.

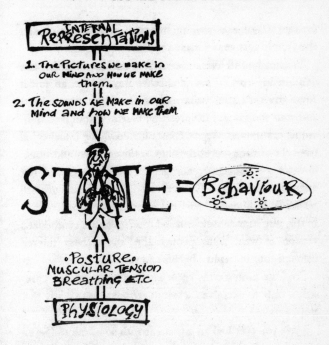

## PHYSIOLOGY

Muscular tension or relaxation, breathing and body posture all influence your state. If your body is tense, it is producing different chemicals from those it produces when it is relaxed, so of course you will feel different.

Your internal representations and physiology are intimately linked in what is called a cybernetic loop. If you change one, this will automatically affect the other. Try smiling when you feel angry. It is hard because your mind is saying one thing and your body another. However, if you manage it you may well be surprised at how much better this simple change can make you *feel*.

In a nutshell all human behaviour is the result of the state you are in – or, to put it another way, we are all under 'state control'. Your behaviour is a manifestation of state and your state is an interpretation based on your own individual experience. We are constantly receiving information from the outside world through our five senses, and therefore we are constantly engaged in making sense of our ongoing experiences. The way we do this, as I mentioned earlier, is to filter and sort the information unconsciously. In this way your conscious mind receives only a synthesized version of what is happening after it has been filtered through your individual beliefs and values.

Since we cannot truly know what reality is and can represent it only to ourselves, why not represent it in a way that empowers us?

Have you ever had an argument with someone and, even hours later, find you keep seeing their face right in front of you and rehear all the nasty things they said to you which made you feel bad? I used to do that until I discovered that if I changed the picture I was looking at and the sounds I was hearing, my feelings instantly changed.

Go ahead and try it for yourself. Think of someone you don't like and notice what you think of. Do you see an image of them, or are you more aware of the sound of their voice? OK, now let's play with the way you are representing them. Try out these changes and notice what happens.

1  Drain out all the colour from the image and make it look like an old black-and-white photograph.

2  Shrink the image.

3  Move the location of the image (if it's on the right move it to the left, or spin it off into space).

4  Give the person a clown's nose, pink hair and Mickey Mouse ears.

5  Move the location of their voice (if it's near, move it further away).

6  Give them a deep sexy voice, or a high-pitched squeaky one, as I suggested for the critical voice earlier.

By making these changes in your internal representations you recode the experience so it no longer triggers the stressful response. You can choose instead simply to be amused.

You can also enhance positive images. Think of something you would really like to happen, imagine how it looks and sounds. Now make the picture bigger and brighter, bring it closer and turn up the volume. Notice how your feelings are instantly changed. You can easily do this in normal waking consciousness as well as in a trance. In our culture we are told *what* to think, but not *how* to think. Many people presume that because there's a voice inside their head they have to listen to it, even if what it says is not supporting them. *You* are in charge of your state and as you read further you will discover more ways to change it.*

*To learn more about techniques in this particular area I recommend that you read *Using your Brain for a Change*, by my friend, Richard Bandler.

The world is a magnificent and exciting place, but we tend to make it seem everyday through our own habituation. This is often a contributory factor in people's problems. By thinking, 'It's just another day like any other' or, 'I know what he's like, he's one of those people', we effectively take our environment, and the people and experiences that are close to us, for granted. Habits are very useful to help us with the tasks in life we need to perform – we don't want to have to waste time or energy thinking about breakfast every morning, so we follow a habit. Unfortunately, habituation can stifle wonder from moment to moment in life, but by sharpening sensory acuity you can attune yourself to experience more of what's going on. Remember, whenever we perceive the world we do so through our filters. We can use hypnosis to choose the filters we use so the world can become a truly enchanting place. But you don't even need to go into a trance to do it. You can start by sharpening your sensory acuity.

This might sound complicated but it really couldn't be simpler. For example, next time you are walking down the street, notice the focus of your vision – staring at the pavement or looking straight ahead of you. Stop and gradually expand your visual awareness. Become aware of what's in the corners of your vision rather than focusing on just one thing. Consciously take it all in, noticing the wealth of colours and shapes. Then feel the contact of the ground beneath you with each footstep and each part of your foot as it touches the ground, then become aware of the air brushing past your body. Listen with curiosity to all the sounds that you weren't paying attention to before – hear when there's sound and when there isn't.

Or, when you are having a conversation with someone you could enjoy noticing as much about them as possible – not just the content of your conversation but all the details of your environment, and the small differences in the face of the person you are talking to, like the little muscular movements in their face. At which subjects do their pupils dilate? When does a smile flicker round their lips? When do they fidget or scratch themselves?

There is always plenty of information in your environment just waiting to be absorbed.

After a while you will automatically begin to experience your environment in new ways, and subsequently your experience of life will become richer. As you notice more, you will discover that you begin to understand more. You will find that each person has characteristic habits and signals which act as a kind of commentary on their behaviour and speech. The more closely you observe which signals correlate with which emotions in each person you talk to, the better and richer your communication will be.

## ASSOCIATIONS

Whenever I go to an airport I begin to feel excited. Even if I am only dropping someone else there, I still get those feelings of delightful anticipation. This is because my mind has many happy *associations* connected with airports: to me they mean travelling to far-off exotic places on exciting adventures. The happy feelings are triggered again by just going to the airport. Some people who travel a great deal on business have negative feelings when they go to an airport – it reminds them of work. The airport itself is neutral; it is the meaning of what we associate it with that produces the reactions.

We are constantly making all kinds of associations with the stimuli that are in our environment and most of them are unconscious. Advertising works largely through association. We associate Michael Jackson with Pepsi, we know that Beanz Meanz Heinz. Some adverts are funny; you laugh and associate that laughter and happy feeling with the product.

Some people only have to use a certain tone of voice and it triggers a different state in you. Some scents or smells, hearing a favourite old love song, seeing a police car in the mirror behind you – all have specific associations that trigger particular states.

It is because every moment of our personal history is recorded in a multi-sensory way that a complete past emotional state can easily be triggered by visual, auditory, kinaesthetic, gustatory or olfactory stimuli in the present. Just seeing an old school photograph can bring back a whole experience of childhood.

Words are triggers for many different kinds of states. The word 'home' elicits one set of associations, whereas the word 'sex' will certainly elicit others. This is because words are labels for things in your experience. For example, in order to understand what coffee is you have to create an internal reminder of the taste for a brief moment. Hypnotists know this and use the power of language to create associations for a subject. Building a rich sensory description of a desired state through language will create a rich sensory experience in the mind of the listener. When I worked as a radio broadcaster we used to say that radio was the theatre of the mind; hypnosis is the ultimate theatre of the mind, with you as the director.

From my career as a DJ I have all kinds of associations with records. Sometimes when I hear a song I suddenly find myself back day-dreaming about a time in the past. I can vividly remember the weather, the faces of my friends, the place I was living, sometimes even the smell of a room. All of the experience is triggered by just one component.

Most performers or athletes have a ritual before a show, race or match, whether they are aware of it or not. Some wear favourite shoes or clothes, others imagine how they want things to go, and some even have lucky mascots. The reason is that these things, through association, put them in a particular state.

The difference between winning and losing can very often be the state you are in. One of the most straight-forward techniques I teach people is how to use association to get into a desired state instantly. Imagine how useful it is for an athlete, entertainer or politician to be able to reach their peak immediately.

Obviously associations can work against you, and indeed most of the limitations people have are the result of associations they make. Some people instantly go into an unresourceful state when it comes to public speaking, others when it comes to intimacy. Extreme examples of external stimuli triggering a powerful negative state are phobias, which are often associations made during moments of great emotional intensity.

The way to change your associations and achieve the state that you want is really very simple. Think of a particular state you desire – let's say it is security. Before you go any further, check to see that it is appropriate for you to reach this new state and that it is congruent with all your values and wishes. Then think of times in the past when you have felt secure. If you have never felt as safe and secure as you would like to, just think about all the benefits of the security you want. Imagine them happening and notice how that makes you feel. Increase the intensity until you feel as secure as you could desire. Build your representation as vividly as you can. Imagine what you will see, hear and feel and how you will behave with your new inner sense of security and then associate it with a particular stimulus. Choose some simple, distinct movement that you can do whenever you need it. An easy and convenient one is to press your thumb and finger together, or you could snap your fingers. When you experience the state at its peak, make this movement to create an association between security and the actions of your fingers.

Open your eyes and change your body posture to mark the end of the procedure, then go back and repeat the whole process again five times in all. The repetition of the process ensures that the association is strong and firm. After a while, you will be able to summon up your feeling of security by repeating that movement. Just that movement, that specific pressure of your thumb and finger, is a concrete, physical trigger which will lead you straight to the feeling you desire.

This is one of the easiest and most effective ways of gaining mastery of whatever state you want. To me this is real magic. There are many variations on this technique – different triggers, different memories, different goals. You may find sounds work better for you than pictures, but whatever the particular elements are that work for you, the basic procedure to follow is laid out in the box overleaf.

A little later on I will show you how to use this technique to combine several states.

## CHANGING YOUR STATE THROUGH REFRAMING QUESTIONS

We are also constantly affecting our state by the questions we ask ourselves. This is because the nature of the conscious mind is to continually analyse, criticize, compare and question. Most of our thinking is made up of the questions we ask and answer ourselves.

Essentially, the results you are currently getting in your life are profoundly influenced by the questions you are asking yourself. Questions help determine the amount of success and failure, of love, fear, anger, joy and wonder, that you experience. If you examine your inner questions, you may be surprised to notice how disempowering some of them are. Some of the people I have worked with were stuck or in pain because they continually asked themselves negatively oriented questions – 'Why *can't* I do this?'

### CREATING THE STATE/YOU WANT

1   Locate the area where you wish to be more resourceful.

2   Decide what state you want – security, happiness, etc.

3   Imagine exactly what it will be like to have the resource state.

4   Build a sensory-rich representation of the resource state – what you will hear, see, feel, etc. You can do this by remembering a time in the past when you experienced this state or imagine what it would be like to be in this state.

5   When you experience the state at its peak, make your association. It can be visual (an image), auditory (a word you say to yourself) or kinaesthetic (a snap of the fingers).

6   Break state by changing your body posture and clearing your mind.

7   Repeat the process five times to strengthen.

8   Test your association by making it again – for example, snap your fingers to check that you go into the desired state.

   If you have any problems just go back over the eight steps.

This question presupposes that you can't. In order to answer it, you have to agree that you can't and so your mind automatically begins to search out all the reasons why that is true.

If, on the other hand, you ask, 'How can I make this work?', the question presupposes something different, that whatever it is can work, and your mind then searches for different information. Changing your state is as easy as asking a new question, because new questions = new answers = new states = new outcomes. If you want to experience better states, ask better questions.

Questions direct your focus and – all together now – You always get more of what you focus on in life. If your quality of life is poor, then one of the factors is almost certainly the questions you are asking. Some examples of common, but unhelpful, questions are:

- Why is life unfair?
- Why does this always happen to me?
- Why don't I like myself?
- Why can't I stop doing $x$?

Think of any area in your life where you are not getting the sort of results you want and say to yourself, 'What are the questions I am asking myself in this area?' Then pose yourself a new question: 'How can I ask this in a way that points towards the positive?' Try asking questions like:

- What is the most elegant way I can solve this problem?
- How many ways of solving this problem can I come up with?

- How can I improve what is most likeable about me?
- How can I most easily stop doing *x*?

These questions make your brain sort for different information and put you in a different, and more resourceful, state. If you are not happy with the answer you get back, then either change the question or ask it again, and keep asking until you are happy. Your brain will carry on searching for you. Sometimes when I have a creative problem I relax into trance, asking my unconscious, 'How many new ways of looking at this can you show me?'

Here is a technique I use every day to put myself in a resourceful state. I simply ask myself these questions:

- What do I have to feel happiest about?
- What in my life can I make even better?
- Who or what in my life makes me feel most loved?
- Who or what in my life makes me feel richest?

As I answer each question I build up a vivid representation of whatever it is I am thinking about – that is, whatever makes me feel good. Then I make an association to that representation (see page 108) by snapping my fingers or pressing my forefinger and thumb together when the representation is at its peak. I make the same association each time I ask one of the questions so I build a super-state. Repeating this for a few days, I essentially programme myself with those resourceful states.

If you go through the ritual of building this super-state each day, it has a powerful cumulative effect and soon you will begin to experience life in a completely different way.

**Some influential characters in the history of hypnotism**

1. Franz Anton Mesmer

2. James Braid

3. Milton H. Erickson

4. Mesmer demonstrates his theory of magnetism at a fashionable gathering.

5. The human plank

6. A typical design for a hypno–disc

7.  Thereses entertains at the Alhambra Music Hall, London.

8.  Paul McKenna, live at the Royal Albert Hall!

## A STEP BY STEP INDUCTION

1. The hypnotist establishes rapport with the subject. He begins giving indirect suggestions by explaining what the subject can expect and pacing her expectations. He has engaged her attention.

2. 'Look up in front of and above you.' He fixates her attention upon a spot on the ceiling.

3. After a while her eyelids become heavy and he instructs her to close them. With the natural relaxation of trance beginning her head also lowers. Eye closure begins.

4. A general relaxation of facial muscles is evidence of her altered state of consciousness. As she continues in trance unconscious resources and abilities are activated.

5. The subject experiences the spontaneous response of her own unconscious to the hypnotist's suggestions. In trance such experiences can be wonderfully vivid and absorbing. As the subject becomes more absorbed in the experience the hypnotist can observe the subject's reaction.

6. The hypnotist suggests her hand is becoming lighter. She experiences her hand as weightless and the upward movement begins to happen without conscious volition.

7. And it continues. Such unconscious movements can end in a static position that can last for up to as long as the trance. This is known as catalepsy.

RAPID INDUCTION In certain contexts a rapid induction is required:

1. The hypnotist directs the subject psychologically towards trance.

2. He compounds this by offering a distraction from the normal conscious visual mind sets.

3. When he senses compliance he tilts her backwards. The shift in all her sensory modalities combined with his verbal suggestion enables the rapid onset of trance.

Instead of manipulating the world to make you feel good, you begin each day feeling the way you want to feel. Don't just take my word for it – try it!

This process is not actually a new invention, but is simply the conscious utilization of a phenomenon that is happening naturally and automatically all the time. My motto is: 'If it's going to happen anyway, let's make it happen the way we want.'


## TRANCES PEOPLE LIVE

The Russian mystic George Ivanovitch Gurdjieff (1866–1949) claimed that we live almost entirely in trance, functioning like machines, along fixed lines of habit. A modern writer who thinks along similar lines is Stephen Wolinsky, whose book *Trances People Live* is an excellent overview of the place and function of trance in everyday life. In traditional hypnosis, trance is viewed as a state induced only by hypnotists. Wolinsky noticed that trance is the means by which symptoms are created and maintained. He observed that all symptoms or problems are glued together by at least one of the classic deep-trance phenomena.

These deep-trance phenomena are used in childhood as ways of surviving the threat of an overwhelming traumatic experience. For example, if a young boy is beaten repeatedly by his father, he lives in fear and his basic reaction will be, 'It hurts, I can't stand this.' In order to survive the experience his unconscious will bring into action a deep-trance phenomenon. He may develop amnesia (it never happened) and/or analgesia (I don't feel a thing). At some point, whichever trance states are most successful in helping him survive the ordeal will begin to function automatically. Twenty years later he arrives for a session with a psychotherapist, complaining that he is terrified of standing up to his boss and feels out of touch with his feelings in relationships.

By the time we are adults we all have automatic clusters of deep-trance phenomena that act as our patterns of defence. For example, fear of public speaking may be created by pseudo-orientation in time – for example, imagining embarrassing outcomes, followed by an unintentional post-hypnotic suggestion in the internal dialogue, 'I can't do it.'

However, not all trances are dysfunctional; some are enjoyable. In the course of a day we enter many trance states. Look at this list of deep-trance phenomena and then we'll see how many of them turn up in the average day.

1  AGE REGRESSION  Remembering or reliving an experience from the past.
2  AGE PROGRESSION  Pseudo-orientation in time, projecting oneself into an imagined future experience.
3  DISASSOCIATION  Detached from an experience as if from the outside.
4  POST-HYPNOTIC SUGGESTION  Internal auditory dialogues.
5  AMNESIA  Forgetting or being unable to remember an experience.

6 NEGATIVE HALLUCINATION Deleting an aspect of experience, not seeing, hearing or feeling something that is there.

7 POSITIVE HALLUCINATION Seeing, hearing or feeling something that is not there.

8 CONFUSION Disorientation, being unclear.

9 TIME DISTORTION Expanding or compressing time.

10 HYPNOTIC DREAMING Fantasizing or day-dreaming.

11 SENSORY DISTORTION Where physical awareness is amplified and sensitized, or dulled and desensitized.

Now let's just run through a typical day.

The alarm goes, triggering *a post-hypnotic suggestion* – 'I must get up' – and *pseudo-orientation in time* – imagining the office environment. On the way into work there is a traffic jam, inducing *time distortion* – the car in front seems to be taking for ever to leave the junction – and *pseudo-orientation in time* – imagining being late, being reprimanded, and from that *regression* – memories of confrontations with authority figures, such as school teachers or parents. You get into work, spot an attractive member of the opposite sex and indulge for a moment in *positive hallucination* – imagining an affair with them. Somebody calls from the other side of the office – *negative hallucination* – but you don't hear while day-dreaming. You get into an argument – *regression* to primitive responses – both parties have a tantrum and fire *post-hypnotic suggestions* at each other – 'You are always messing up', 'You are always picking on me.' You go outside to have a cigarette to calm down

– *disassociation* from feelings. You go back to work and *pseudo-orientation in time* – imagining the future of the project – and conclude with a *post-hypnotic suggestion* – 'I know how to get this to work.' Time to go home – *negative hallucination* – you can't find car keys, search and find they were right in front of you all the time.

I have touched only the tip of the iceberg with this little scenario, but a generalized version of events like this does give a simple overview of the situation. Obviously, though, for each individual the complexity of these trances and partial trances, and their interaction, is far too complicated to present in an abbreviated list form like this because there are just so many permutations at so many different levels.

As a way of freeing yourself from the automatism of this process, Wolinsky recommends what he calls the act of *witnessing* – 'Stepping outside of your problem to observe it, you create a larger context for it.' It is not splitting your mind into two parts, one matching the other; it is the unifying of the small you, of attachments and problems, and the larger you – that is, the context within which your experience takes place. He has an excellent technique that helps you to spot your own trances and consequently other people's. Most important, it moves you towards witnessing and beyond the identifications of your everyday trances. The following exercises are based on Wolinsky's methods of understanding and transforming your own everyday trance.

EXERCISE ONE

1   Make yourself comfortable.

2   Watch your mind, noticing the internal pictures and
    internal dialogue it creates.

3   Detach yourself and simply observe it.

EXERCISE TWO

Repeat Exercise One, then begin to label each thought or
picture with the appropriate deep-trance phenomenon
description. For example, if you think of a past event, label
it 'regression'.

EXERCISE THREE

After you have managed to do Exercise Two, consciously
create the deep-trance phenomenon that is occurring. For
example, if a picture from the past comes up, label it
'regression' and then intentionally create several copies of
the picture, look at them and let them go. If you hear an
internal voice re-create what it is saying several times. The
same applies to feelings.

After a while you will begin to realize that you are not
your trances; you are, in fact, the *creator* of them, and by
intentionally creating them several times in the present you
will learn how to control them. What you are left with is
*you*, the observer and creator of your experience.

This concept is the basis of some Eastern religious practices and can be taken to extremes with fascinating results. One Thai Buddhist master recommends 'self-awareness' as the way to end 'suffering which is caused by greed and desires'. He calls this the 'study of dharma' – basically the study of self, which is 'the observation of feelings and thoughts'. His teachings go beyond the simple mind techniques that I have shown you and include 'self-awareness' in every body movement. 'When it moves, know that it moves. When it ends, know that it ends.'

For beginners, he suggests a gradual effort to be aware of physical movement in daily activities.

When you raise your hand, know that you do. When you flip the palm of your hand, know that too. Know it when you walk forward and backward, when turning left and right. When looking downward or upward, or when the eyelids move or when the mouth is opening, when breathing in and breathing out. Be aware.

He then applies this philosophy to the mind, explaining that, while watching body movements, thoughts will arise. He advises letting them pass and practising just watching your thoughts. He believes that by thinking thoughts you are trapped in them, identifying with them. He teaches people to see their thoughts and not to try to eradicate them but to become a detached observer. This can be done by anybody. After constant practice it is said to lead to a state of liberation and oneness. This may not be true for everyone but these apparently simple mind and 'trance-watching' exercises can be the beginning of the path to enlightenment and freedom from the second-hand trances of our prefabricated 'culture'.

# 7

# Self-hypnosis

We all have the ability to hypnotize ourselves. This is wonderful for relaxation, problem-solving and overall personal enhancement. Rather than being hypnotized by someone else, in self-hypnosis your own conscious mind is the hypnotist.

Learning self-hypnosis is a bit like learning to ride a bicycle – at first you think you don't know how to do it, but you just have to keep trying. You start, fall off, pick yourself up and try again, and all of a sudden, sooner than you think, you discover you've ridden a fair way without knowing how you did it. Trance is like that – you find you can go into trance after you've spent some time trying and suddenly it just happens, even though you don't know quite how. Like any skill, it requires practice, but when you've mastered it you have a resource which is yours for ever.

In everyday life we drift into natural trances by focusing our attention – day-dreaming, looking at clouds or watching the fire. This often coincides with the ultradian rest phase, referred to earlier.

It's very easy and perfectly safe to use hypnosis. Some people let their acquired fears about hypnosis stop them from fully experiencing the state, while others just try too hard. There is a lovely story about Milton Erickson, who was out walking one day when he found a horse roaming free. He jumped on it and off it went, past one farm, then another, and another, before finally turning in at the fourth farm. The farmer came up to him and thanked him for returning the horse, but was puzzled that he knew which farm to take it to. Erickson said, 'I didn't, but the horse knew. I just went with it and let it take me where it was going.'

Trance is like that – you don't have to try to get it right; just notice where it takes you. Stand out of the way and let it happen. It is similar to the experience of trying to get to sleep in that the harder you try, the more awake you stay – what's called the law of reverse effort. By counting sheep or reading, conscious attention is diverted away from sleep and so the loop of reverse effort is broken. The same can happen with self-hypnosis; the secret is just to let it happen. Avoid over-analysing and instead simply notice the experience. In self-hypnosis you become both hypnotist and subject. You find something to focus on – say, a physical object like a spot on the ceiling – or start counting numbers backwards, which will distract your conscious mind – the left brain or logical, critical part. This is essentially what the hypnotist does. Meanwhile, at the same time, like a good subject, you become involved in the process, relaxing and noticing any thoughts and bodily sensations.

## SAFETY AND CONTEXT

The five primary stages of self-hypnosis are:

1   **PREPARE YOUR PHYSICAL COMFORT**   Make your-
    self comfortable – possibly remove contact lenses,
    loosen your collar, go to the toilet, etc.
2   **SET BOUNDARIES**   Set a purpose for the trance –
    relaxation and energy regeneration, problem-solving,
    etc.
3   **SET TIME**   Set a time limit for your trance and ensure
    that you will not be disturbed. It doesn't actually
    cause any harm if you are, but it is just as uncomfort-
    able as being awoken abruptly from ordinary sleep.
4   **SET SAFETY CATCH**   Create a safety statement for
    your protection.

It is best to create your own statement, setting clear and
precise boundaries of what you wish to accomplish in
trance. For example,

I am going to go into a trance for the next twenty
minutes. During that time I am going to do $x$ in order to
$y$. If during this time anything should call into question
my continued health and well-being, or if for any reason
or emergency I need to, I will immediately return to
normal waking consciousness with all the resources I
need to deal effectively with the situation. At the end of
my twenty-minute trance I will awake, having
accomplished my task with a sense of energy and
refreshment.

Remember, you are always ultimately in control of your experience. No one has ever been unable to come out of a trance. Going into trance and coming out are as natural as sleeping and waking.

## 5 START INDUCTION

## VARIOUS SELF-HYPNOSIS INDUCTIONS

### Mrs Erickson's Induction

This is my personal favourite self-induction method. Mrs Erickson is highly adept at going into altered states and invented this technique after learning how to go into trance with her husband.

### TECHNIQUE

First make yourself comfortable and find something to focus your vision on. Then make four statements about your *visual* experience. For example,

In front of me I can see the books. I can see the floor. I can see the wall. I can see the cuffs of my shirt at the periphery of my vision.

Then move to your *auditory* experience – what you can hear – and make four statements to yourself about that. For example,

Now I am aware that I hear the traffic passing on the road. I can hear my breathing. I hear the ticking of the clock and the birdsong outside.

Then move to your *kinaesthetic* experience – what you can feel – and make four statements to yourself about that. For example,

Now I am aware that I feel the weight of my body in the chair. I can feel my facial muscles relaxing. I can feel the warmth of my hands resting on my thighs. I can feel the movement of my shirt over my chest as it rises and falls with my breathing.

Then, while maintaining your point of focus, return to the visual channel of awareness and make three statements about your ongoing visual experience. This isn't a test of inventiveness, so it doesn't matter at all if you repeat yourself; just tell yourself exactly what you are experiencing at the time. Next describe your auditory experience with three more statements, whatever you are actually hearing. Then make three statements about your kinaesthetic experience. Go round again, with two statements about each sensory awareness, and finally one statement about each. At some point your eyes will feel tired. Close them and continue making statements about your ongoing experience, although the visual representations you may be most aware of with your eyes closed will probably be from your imagination. You can carry on with these internal descriptions just as effectively, finding increasingly finer descriptions within your sensory experience. For example, 'Now I am aware I see a glass. . . Now I am aware that there is water in it. . . Now I am aware that the water is fizzy. . . Now I am aware that I see a reflection in the glass.'

What you are creating is a biofeedback loop. You are feeding back to yourself your own experience, which sends you into an altered state.

| | |
|---|---|
| Now I am aware that I see | × 4 |
| Now I am aware that I hear | × 4 |
| Now I am aware that I feel | × 4 |
| | |
| Now I am aware that I see | × 3 |
| Now I am aware that I hear | × 3 |
| Now I am aware that I feel | × 3 |
| | |
| Now I am aware that I see | × 2 |
| Now I am aware that I hear | × 2 |
| Now I am aware that I feel | × 2 |
| | |
| Now I am aware that I see | × 1 |
| Now I am aware that I hear | × 1 |
| Now I am aware that I feel | × 1 |

When you begin to feel a little fatigued, just close your eyes and go inside. If you get to the bottom of the list and find that your conscious mind still wishes to be active, you can return to the top and find increasingly finer distinctions within your sensory experience, until you begin to feel that fatigue. This is also an excellent way to overcome insomnia.

*Nested-images Induction*

An excellent induction devised by my fellow hypnotist Michael Breen, this is for those who enjoy and are good at visualizing or enjoy getting better at visualizaiton.

**TECHNIQUE**

1 Make yourself comfortable and close your eyes.

2 Call to mind an image of how you would look if you were quite relaxed.

3 Step into that image and experience what it's like to be relaxed. See with those eyes, hear with those ears, and feel those feelings.

4 From within that image imagine what it would be like to be twice as relaxed. See with those eyes, hear with those ears, feel those feelings of relaxation.

5 Step into that image and experience what it is like to be that relaxed.

6 From within that image imagine what it would be like to feel even more relaxed.

7 Step inside that image and really experience what it would be like. See with those eyes, etc.

Carry on until you achieve an experience that satisfies your personal criteria for success in self-hypnosis.

This is an excellent technique for creating states that might be difficult to access in one fell swoop – this refers to any state, be it happiness, motivation, ecstasy or whatever. Again it feeds back to you your present experience and then targets where you want to go, a little at a time. Remember, you can accomplish anything if you break it down into small enough chunks.

You can use Michael's technique for getting into any particular state by breaking it down into stepping stones. So, for example, you might choose to go from *apathetic* to *neutral* to *interested* to *pleased* to *happy* to *excited* to *ecstatic*! You can use any number of links to go from one state to another, and this is an excellent technique for designing the kind of experiences you want to have.

### Systematic Relaxation

This is a classic self-hypnosis induction. Although it can take longer than others, it can be profoundly relaxing, to a point where loss of bodily awareness occurs.

#### TECHNIQUE

Make yourself comfortable, sitting or lying down, and suggest to yourself either out loud or internally that you are going to relax your jaw. As you relax your jaw, next relax the muscles around your mouth, then the muscles in and around your nose, taking it slowly and steadily, relaxing your cheeks, and then your forehead, next the muscles around your eyes, and all around the top of your head. Relax the muscles at the side of your head, then the back of your head, and then your neck and the muscles behind your eyes. Relax your shoulders, your upper back and your chest. Relax your torso and let the relaxation spread down through your arms to your fingers, from your legs all the way to your feet, down to the very tips of your toes.

You can do it in even more detail if you want. For example, feeling the weight, warmth and shape of each finger as it relaxes.

This systematic relaxation is a yogic practice, and is used for stress management or a guided meditation. Once again, this process focuses your attention and uses repetition and monotony to take you into an altered state.

## Counting Backwards

### TECHNIQUE

This can be combined with other approaches as it distracts the conscious mind through monotony and overloading. While you relax your body as previously described, simply being counting backwards from 100 in 3s, making each number a different colour as you imagine it.

## Self-hypnosis through Imagination

A hypnotic trance can be induced and enhanced through the use of mental imagery.

TECHNIQUES

One of the classic scenarios is to imagine you are walking down a staircase and, with each step you take, you relax more and go deeper into trance. Written on each step is the word 'relax'. This can be combined with many of the techniques below, or used as a gentle introduction to a further induction.

Similarly, you can imagine you are on an escalator. Once again the metaphorical implication is that the further down you go, the deeper into trance you progress and the more profoundly you relax, or the greater the feeling of well-being.

Imagery is one of the ways that human beings think and process information. Everybody dreams and can visualize. Some people maintain that they cannot visualize, but if I ask you what your favourite shirt looks like, in order to answer that question you have to go to an internal picture for the information.

In order to have success with self hypnosis, it is important to use your imagination. Like any new skill you wish to master, just take it one step at a time, breaking it into smaller and smaller chunks. You don't have to think of an elaborate scenario all at once. Pick out one thing and imagine it, begin to see as much detail as you can and don't be too surprised as you begin to see more. Trance is a state of fascination with one thing at a time.

The left brain (the seat of the conscious mind) is constantly judging and evaluating, comparing and looking for differences; it is always 'reality-testing'. The right brain (the seat of the unconscious) is associational and non-linear, and is imaginative rather than logical. In hypnosis it is important to suspend analysis and criticism and become involved in your imagination. Some people want to check constantly whether they are hypnotized or not, and that is a function of the conscious mind.

Children are great at going in trances, imagining wonderful far-away places. This is because they have not developed the conscious faculty of critical thinking to the extent of an adult. However, in our culture many children are conditioned away from right-brain thinking by messages like, 'Stop day-dreaming' or, 'There is no such person as Father Christmas.' Self hypnosis is often easier when you remember how you used to use your imagination when you were younger.

When you suspend reality-testing and become involved in what you are imagining, you perceive whatever you are imagining as reality. If you think of your favourite food vividly enough, your mouth will begin to water. That is because the mind and the body are intimately linked. In the same way, the more vividly you imagine a wonderful relaxing time you had on holiday, the more you re-create all the internal feelings and benefits you had for yourself.

The imagination can also work against us – phobias are a good example. Any disappointment in life does require imaginative pre-planning – you have imagined events taking a certain course and when they don't you feel bad about it. The process is intensified by finding finer and finer sensory information.

## Repetition

An altered state can be induced through repetition of a word – a popular practice in many of the Eastern religions. The word for this is mantra, meaning 'thought' in Sanskrit. The repetition can be of any sound or movement or picture. When something is done or said for the first time, the conscious mind processes and reality-tests it, but if it is repeated the reality-testing becomes unnecessary and the stimulus moves out of your conscious awareness and is monitored by the unconscious.

We have all witnessed this phenomenon before. As an example, think of how someone who lives near a railway track doesn't notice the trains, but you do if you go round to visit. The conscious mind tends to ignore repetitive sounds, leaving them to the unconscious. In Nichiren Shoshu Buddhism the chanting of a mantra is a key principle. The mantra has a specific meaning and significance for each individual. After initial repetition the mantra is monitored by, and implanted into, the unconscious through the bombardment of repetition.

Remember the golden rule, 'You always get more of what you focus on. That focus can be conscious or unconscious. So by continually focusing upon the mantra you get whatever the mantra means to you. Some people chant for a partner, some for enlightenment. In transcendental meditation the word you are given is supposed to be of particular significance to the meditator.

The same applies to music. The rhythm of many pop records is repetitive, and the message in the lyrics impacts upon your unconscious. I am not suggesting that you get hypnotized by listening to a record, but continual exposure to a particular message does impinge upon your consciousness.

Many records nowadays are about how he or she broke my heart; some suggest violence or even perverse sexual ideas. If you are continually exposed to these messages, there can be an effect.

TECHNIQUE

By continually suggesting an idea to yourself like 'I am relaxing', after a while you will. State what you want, and state it in the positive. For example, if you say, 'I am *not* tense', your focus is upon being tense. Say instead, 'I am relaxing more and more.' *This is very important!* In order to 'not' something, you first of all have to focus on what it is. Say your mantra or affirmation out loud or silently to yourself over and over until you are bored, then continue saying it! Notice, but disregard, any thoughts that come into your mind. You will soon become aware of an enjoyable and relaxed shift inwards. If you find yourself forgetting the mantra, just start again. Remember, it is an effortless process.

*Self-hypnosis through Changing Physiology*

If you make certain changes in your concentration between mind and body, you change your internal awareness.

## TECHNIQUES

Change your breathing patterns. Usually a few deep breaths is enough to make shifts in your awareness. Avoid excessive inhalation and exhalation (hyperventilation) because they over-oxygenate the blood and can cause dizziness and even loss of consciousness. Breathing from the diaphragm, the muscle at the bottom of your ribcage is recommended.

Another powerful technique is to take in a deep breath and, while holding it, tighten every muscle in your body – feet, legs, arms, stomach and face. Then after a few seconds release the breath at the same time as you relax all the muscles. The tension before makes the relaxation more profound – a bit like pushing down hard on a metal spring and then suddenly releasing it.

Another method is to look up at where your eyebrows are for about fifteen to twenty seconds, then stop, relax and close your eyes. This serves two purposes: it creates a slight strain, so it makes the relaxation greater, and it also releases a burst of alpha waves in the brain.

### Self-hypnosis through Tapes

As I have already said, there are plenty of hypnosis or quasi-hypnosis tapes available nowadays, but it is also a good idea for you to record your own self-hypnosis tapes.

Obviously you'll need a machine, tapes and a little bit of practice. I suggest that you speak at about a third of your normal speed and leave plenty of time for your instructions to be followed. Remember that there has to be an element of monotony and repetition in your induction to make it effective. It's best to make the recording without too many stops and starts in it, so that it flows smoothly. You may find that it takes you several attempts to get it absolutely right, but that's part of the fun. Don't worry if you are a little self-conscious about your voice at first; most people are, and you will soon get used to it.

Play the tape as often as you need to feel comfortable. When I make one I usually play it about three times a week. I might set time aside during the day to listen to it, or play it as I drift off to sleep at night. I gave a simple induction script earlier in the book (page 51) which you might like to use as a framework for your own tape.

## THE STRUCTURE OF SELF-HYPNOSIS

1  STATEMENT OF INTENTION  During the next twenty minutes I am going into trance in order to do $x$. If for any good reason or emergency I need to, I will awake instantly. I will rest deeply in trance and awake refreshed, relaxed and alert in twenty minutes.

2  CONTENT OF TRANCE  The suggestions you wish to offer yourself – I am feeling more confident! I now imagine myself more confident!

3  WAKING UP  A suggestion to return to normal waking consciousness – As I count back from five to one I will awake refreshed and fully alert.

I have explained a number of different techniques separately, but you can use any combination of them to create the one(s) that are particularly suited to you. However, always stick to the structure outlined above. Have fun!

# 8

# Past and Future Lives

> 'We can never finally know; I simply believe that some part of the human self or soul is not subject to the laws of space and time.'
>
> Carl Jung

## PAST-LIFE REGRESSION

Recently there has been a lot of interest in hypnotic past-life regression – past-life regression is making a comeback, as it were! This is a controversial subject. Sceptics require concrete proof that what subjects have experienced is really a past life and not just the product of an over-active imagination. It is hard enough to believe that hypnosis can take a person back to the minutest details of their own life, let alone to the life of another person who is now dead, but that is precisely what past-life regression claims to do.

The hypnotist puts subjects into trance and then takes them back and back and back through time to past centuries; back and back, all the while suggesting that they stop at whatever period of time they feel comfortable in. The hypnotist will then ask the subjects to go over details of the life that they find themselves in. If a person has regressed to Africa then he or she would most likely speak and understand the language of that country, and this is the easiest way to verify if what they are describing is real or just fantasy.

There have been famous cases, such as Bridie Murphy's, of what appeared to be clear proof of past lives that were later convincingly challenged. Bridie's nurse in her early years was an Irish woman whose own history was remarkably similar to the 'past life' that Bridie 'recalled' under hypnosis. However, in hypnotherapy perhaps the ability to prove regression doesn't matter. If it helps somebody to overcome a problem in this life by visiting a past life, the process definitely has therapeutic value.

There are six main theories to explain what past-life regression may be.

## Life after Death

This is the most commonly held idea, based on the theory of reincarnation that says, quite simply, these people have lived past lives and, although they have cast off the shell of the dead person, their soul or spirit has lived on and come back again in another body. Under hypnosis this spirit's 'memory' then recalls details of past lives it has lived.

A related theory is the one held by spiritualists that says the life force of a human being who has died actually enters a living person under hypnosis, providing details for that person to channel.

### The Collective Unconscious

This theory is derived from Carl Jung's notion of the unconscious. It is held that the past experience of the human race is incorporated into the brain structure of a human being and each person inherits this when they are born. This experience is condensed into typical modes of behaviour and different personality types that greatly influence the conscious mind of every individual. In this way we are all playing parts consisting of all the characteristics of a personal and collective unconscious, and many different personas may well be stored within the human brain, all capable of being accessed through hypnosis. This theory does not, however, explain the fact that certain subjects when regressed produce accurate historical data.

### Cosmic Memory

This theory is loosely derived from the first law of thermodynamics, which states that heat is a form of energy and energy cannot be manufactured or destroyed, only changed. The brain waves formed by the human brain are essentially a form of energy and if they cannot be destroyed, then they must exist in some way somewhere. The cosmic-memory theory contends that these brain waves continue to exist rather like long-wave radio signals and are then picked up or tuned into by another brain while in trance.

## Parallel-Universe Theory

If you thought the idea of the cosmic memory was difficult to follow, this is even more complicated. To understand it you first need to understand the quantum theory which states that the atomic world is irrational and that subatomic particles like the electron don't follow any predetermined pattern but are unpredictable. This basically means that our solid and familiar world is actually just a muddle of incomprehensible particles.

Based upon this theory comes the idea of parallel universes, which states that for every movement of an atomic or subatomic particle an infinite number of different movements could have taken place. If each movement is equally likely or unlikely, then each must have in fact happened. This would mean that alongside our universe is an infinite number of parallel universes, just as real as our own, with people as real as we think we are. Is there another world where Madonna is a nun or Margaret Thatcher is still prime minister. Who knows?

## Telepathy

More science fiction? Maybe, but pause a moment and ask yourself how many times you have been thinking of somebody only to have them ring up moments later. What about when you say something at the same time as somebody else and then realize you were both thinking the same thing, or you dream the same dream as someone close to you, or experience feelings of *déjà vu*? There have been many cases of supposed past-life regression where the subject seems to have read the mind of somebody else in the room.

## Genetically Inherited Memory

This final theory is an extension of the idea of inheritance. The genes you inherit from your parents determine the way that you look. The theory proposes that they also pass on some sort of 'encoded memory' that can be accessed in a deeply relaxed state. The animal kingdom offers some evidence that this could be possible. How else would birds know to fly south in the winter, perhaps to the exact nesting places of their parents? How else would squirrels know to bury nuts in the winter or hedgehogs to hibernate or salmon to return to their birthplace to spawn? Perhaps the personae that people access when they are regressed are in fact those of their own ancestors?

Past-life regression has helped an enormous number of people, who claim it is a very mind-opening experience. I have heard people speak in foreign languages they have never spoken before and recount details of places and events for which there is no logical explanation.

If you are interested in taking this further, let me offer a few words of caution first. Often past-life regression can be an excuse for sensationalist over-stimulation of the imagination. It might be worth wondering what is lacking in your own life to make you want to play with a different one? What do you need to do to make this life more rewarding and enjoyable?

If it comes up in therapy, remember you are living here and now and it is here and now that you must find the solutions you need. Don't let yourself be distracted by past traumas, real or imagined, your own or others', from the work of healing you can do here and now.


## FUTURE-LIFE PROGRESSION

A large number of people nowadays understand the concept of past-life regression and even accept it as a possibility, but there is much more resistance to the idea of future-life progression. Recently the subject has come to the fore of popular interest, due largely to my friend Dr Chet Snow's best-selling book *Dreams of the Future*.

In his book Dr Snow documents hundreds of hypnotic sessions where subjects have been taken into their future lives at specific periods between 2100 and 2500 AD. Through hypnotic progression he has uncovered stunning evidence of agreement between historical prophecies from around the world and the accounts of over two thousand subjects taken on these psychic voyages.

Primarily, the difficulty people have in understanding and accepting the concept of future-life progression stems from the Western world's view of time as linear. We see the past as what has already happened, as fixed, and the future as changeable as it has not yet occurred. However, in some Eastern cultures time is seen as circular, so that things are endlessly repeated. This may be pretty difficult to get your head around, but put simply the premise is that events that happened in the past shape the future. This is best explained in Dr Snow's book:

Perhaps the best description of cyclical Time belongs to the nineteenth-century German philosopher Georg F. Hegel. He described man's Time perception as that of someone slowly climbing a winding mountain path. Imagine, he said, a cone-shaped mountain rising from a flat plain. A spiral pathway winds around the mountain from its base toward its peak. As one climbs up the mountain one necessarily returns to the same side again and again, although each time from a slightly higher level.

Consequently the traveler whose gaze is fixed on the plain below will periodically see the same landmarks return to view, cycle after cycle, while he who looks only straight down at the path ahead will continually see new ground in front of him. For the former it may take generations to realize that although the same landmarks reappear, they do so from a new, higher perspective each time, implying that Time is progressive not eternally repetitious. He who sees only the ground immediately ahead may never realize that in fact his path is marked by prior similar experiences. The wise man will understand that his progress up the mountain may be predicted and assisted by carefully observing both the periodic return of specific major landmarks below and the roughness or smoothness of the pathway currently being walked.

The same obviously applies to the student of future predictions. While remaining ever aware of the newness of each turn of Time's wheel, it is important to review what former sages have correctly predicted and to compare their landmarks with those currently in view. It is thus that one becomes aware of just how cyclical human history really has been despite clear evidence of cultural progress as well.

Thus time has two qualities: events do happen in an order and sequence (linear) and are also determined by what has gone before (cyclical).

The most fascinating thing about his research was that out of more than two thousand people hypnotized and taken into 'the future', the vast majority – 98 per cent – had incredibly similar experiences in the progressions they described. The four basic scenarios were humanity living in New Age-style settlements, high-tech cities dependent on artificial environments, primitive isolated survivor communities and space-farers.

The reason that they report similar experiences could indeed be because they are able to access timelessness through their unconscious mind, where all time happens *now*, so past, present and future exist simultaneously; or perhaps they are just bringing to the surface the human race's deepest-rooted beliefs about the future. Either way in one important sense it amounts to the same thing. As Dr Snow himself says about the hypnotic progressions in his book, 'Parts of the mass dreams of the future that we have on Earth are projecting our subconscious minds today; as such they are important harbingers of what we may consciously be living through tomorrow.'

Although Dr Snow recounts what many subjects experience several hundred years from now, of more immediate interest are the accounts of events leading up to and just after the end of the millennium (the year 2000). He reports dramatic social, economic and geophysical changes that seem to be affecting the world within the next few years.

It is absolutely fascinating to see that some of the predictions that these subjects made in the early 1980s have already begun to come true. The predictions include the fall of Communism in the Eastern Bloc, civil war in Yugoslavia, significant inflation in food prices, extreme and unusual weather patterns that cause havoc with crops and livestock production, scarcity of petrol, personal finance and credit problems, instability in the stock market followed by financial crisis, scarcity of money in general and the widespread use of barter for personal transactions.

Serious geophysical changes include major volcanic activity, sea quakes and the sinking of land, with much of California and Japan disappearing altogether. Extra political tensions are also prophesied, with nations scrambling to maintain their current living standards in the face of the problems – 'The culmination of natural and man-made disasters that together wipe out large numbers of people in a relatively short order.' The good news is that global nuclear war is *not* foreseen.

Of course, these prophecies are not in essence new. There are numerous historical predictions that match accurately the times we are now passing through. The predictions of Nostradamus, the Hopi Indians, the Bible and

Edgar Cayce all bear some resemblance to those in *Dreams of the Future*.

Dr Snow's view is that, 'Although we tend to be culturally hypnotized by powerful, global psychic archetypes such as the Apocalypse, it does not represent the only vision of our planetary future.' Indeed what we see in such cases need not be considered a rigidly fixed and predetermined future, but the most probable outcome of all the untold multitudes of choices taken by humanity so far, and the projection of the collective beliefs of humanity at the moment.

Having heard what could be in store for us in the future, I decided to investigate in my own personal future. Dr Snow describes this as a snapshot of karma, and put in that frame the idea instantly appealed. I went into a trance and he suggested that I was going three hundred years into the future, to another incarnation, in which I found, much to my amazement, that I was a woman! The experience of a pregnancy and birth have certainly given me a different perspective on my life, as indeed being in a female body and life did. Whether it was real or just my vivid imagination I have no way of knowing. Was I really in the future or was it just a learning metaphor constructed by my unconscious to help me in understanding myself and others? The bottom line is that it doesn't matter. It was a truly fascinating voyage.

If you want to find out more about future-life progression, I recommend that you seek out Dr Chet Snow's book. It makes truly remarkable reading and certainly

opened my eyes to the possibilities that may well be in store
for us.

# 9

# Modern Hypnosis

## MILTON H. ERICKSON

By the time of his death in 1980, Milton Erickson was acknowledged as the world's foremost medical hypnotist and psychotherapist. As I have already said, before Erickson hypnotists had mostly been authoritarian in approach, giving commands to the patient. He became the master of *indirect* hypnosis and was consequently able to succeed where other therapists had failed. Erickson was well known for his writings on hypnosis, and many books have also been written about him, analysing his work and the invaluable contribution he made to modern psychotherapy. His work also formed the foundations for some of today's popular psychology movements. In this chapter and the next I will demonstrate the importance of his contribution. More than anybody else, he has shown brilliantly the enormous potential of hypnosis.

Milton Erickson was struck by polio twice in his life and in his later years was confined to a wheelchair. He was colourblind, tone deaf and dyslexic. Yet he managed to overcome these disabilities, as well as help others overcome a huge variety of other problems, by using straightforward hypnotic techniques. Erickson even managed to control the physical pain he was in most of the time through self-hypnosis. Indeed, his disabilities and the incidents of his unusual personal history gave him a unique perspective on life.

The basis of Erickson's therapy was to find out how patients thought, and then meet them at their own level. Many therapists, even today, operate from a rigid set of beliefs and ideals. They work at installing their personal understanding and model of happiness in their clients. Erickson was able to achieve astonishing results consistently because he used the client's model of the world to guide the therapy. He believed that a suggestion would not work properly unless it was compatible with the unconscious needs of the patient.

Although Erickson was an accomplished hypnotist, he was first and foremost a psychotherapist and employed a number of tactics in helping people to change. He was able to bypass any conscious resistance to his suggestions by being 'indirect'; he would communicate his suggestions during what seemed like just a casual conversation.

There are six major components to his method of hypnotic communication: tonality and marking; language; presupposition; ambiguity; metaphor; and rapport. Erickson also observed these patterns in his clients. People frequently mark out portions of their communication unconsciously with a gesture, a change of voice tone or expression. They are often unknowingly telling you something at another level.

## Tonality and Marking

In any communication over 90 per cent consists of voice tonality and body language, with only a small proportion being the actual words used. What we say is, remarkably, not as important as how we say it. In the analysis of speech, our conscious attention is predominantly focused upon content, or what is being said. Erickson would mark out sections of his spoken communication by changing his voice pitch or through hestitations. For example:

'I don't want you to *go into a trance* until *you want to*.'

In this way the meaning of the emphasized words goes straight into the unconscious mind.

## Language

### PRESUPPOSITION

He cleverly constructed his language to make it highly influential. For example:

'Would you like to go into a trance now or in a few moments.'

This in effect presupposes, presumes, that the client will go into a trance whichever option they choose.

*Ambiguity*

He was artful at being vague. Look at the following:

> 'And you can find those resources that help you in those ways that you want them too, even the ones you are not necessarily aware of yet. . .'

This kind of ambiguity allows a subject to hallucinate whatever their specific needs and answers are. This is one of the ways Erickson would help a client to elicit appropriate information, just as politicians manage to give the impression that they have answered a question by using vague and ambiguous phrases, allowing listeners to imagine the meaning.

*Metaphors*

Erickson was a genius in his use of metaphors and stories. As clients listened to one of Erickson's stories with their conscious mind, their unconscious mind would receive the benefit of the underlying meaning of the story. Metaphors would allow listeners to view a situation in a new and non-threatening way. Whenever we explain an idea by likening it to something else, we are using a metaphor. They are symbols and create emotional intensity. Stories that teach and heal people have been around for thousands of years – think of the stories told by Jesus, or the Sufi stories, or the Zen koans.

We all use metaphors constantly to describe our state of being to ourselves and to others: 'I'm in the dark', 'Life is a bed of roses', 'It's an uphill struggle', 'It's a jungle out there.' The metaphors people choose tell you a lot about the way their world is constructed. For some people life is a 'game', while for others it is a 'battle'. I used to work with a man who was obsessed with football, and consequently his language was loaded with footballing metaphors. It helped me create a deeper sense of understanding with him by using his way of looking at the world. I would say that I was going to 'tackle' the problem because I was in the 'right position', and helping the rest of 'the team' was my immediate 'goal'.

Erickson would listen to the metaphors a client used to help him elicit their view of the world and then tell an apparently simple story that helped to change their perspective. The metaphors he used were more than just stories, of course; they were symbols with several levels of meaning.

Take a typical example of how he would deal with a married couple's sexual problems. He would choose something in their lives that was *analogous* to sex. For example, while having a conversation about something else, he might appear to be distracted into talking about having dinner together and discuss how women like appetizers while men with big appetites often prefer to dive in to the meat and potatoes; how some people might enjoy a more leisurely dinner while others just want the meal over with. If his patients began to connect what he was talking about with sexual relations he would quickly change the subject.[1]

In order for his messages to be effective they needed to be outside conscious awareness. He might end the conversation talking about something completely different. Although such use of metaphor seems fairly transparent explained like this, a skilful hypnotist would avoid letting his or her patient make this obvious connection, so that it would be made instead at an unconscious level and lead to an apparently autonomous change in behaviour.

## Rapport

Erickson was a meticulous student of human behaviour and one of the most effective tools he used to gain trust and understanding with his clients was his ability to create rapport swiftly. He would carefully match his voice tonality, breathing and gestures with each individual (in the manner I described in my section 'Rapport' (pages 29–33). Since these things are also mostly outside conscious awareness, he would be creating his bonding with each person directly at the unconscious level.

Erickson appreciated that hypnosis is not necessarily like a switch you can turn on and off. For some people it is more like a path, where effects are cumulative. I have highlighted some of the different aspects of Erickson's behaviour in isolation, but it was the *overall* pattern of his communication that created his amazing results.

Compared with many of the psychological techniques practised today, Milton Erickson used a lot more *practical* ways of healing. He didn't hold with the traditional psychoanalytical methods of digging into a patient's past and understanding the origins of a problem; he felt that this knowledge didn't necessarily guarantee a cure. Instead of being interested in the content or story of a person's problem, he was more concerned with how the problem or behaviour 'helped' the individual and what purpose it served. Erickson understood that the unconscious mind is not logical but *purposeful*. Often an individual will develop an illness to avoid having to confront something. People who get sore throats before having to speak publicly could well be being protected by their unconscious because they remember when they were humiliated talking in front of the class as a child.

Most important of all, Milton Erickson believed that people are not 'broken', and that all human behaviour, no matter how inappropriate, serves a purpose and in some way helps us. So rather than try to eliminate the undesired behaviour, he would acknowledge it and find the person an alternative way of accomplishing the same purpose. He moved one client's paralysis from one arm to another and eventually to her fingernails. She could have her paralysis, but it did not interfere with her life.

As Erickson's work became better known, many people went to Phoenix to witness his magic. These days there are Ericksonian societies located around the world where people who are attracted to his work share ideas. There is an ever increasing number of therapists practising Ericksonian hypnosis. Among those who flocked to see him in Phoenix were two men interested in understanding and establishing how he achieved his results, Richard Bandler and John Grinder.

## NEURO-LINGUISTIC PROGRAMMING

Neuro–linguistic programming (NLP), the new psychology of personal excellence, is one of the most important tools in psychology today. It came largely from the skills and understandings of Milton Erickson, as studied and codified in the 1970s by Richard Bandler, a mathematician and computer scientist, and John Grinder, a prominent linguist, both of whom had backgrounds in therapy. Their aim was to understand the patterns of highly effective people in therapy, education and business. Together they studied individuals in these fields and mapped step by step how they got their results.

Often the important elements of a particular skill are unconscious for the person possessing the ability. Bandler and Grinder used a process called 'modeling' to understand and format the internal states, feelings, behaviours and physiology that produced highly effective communication and changes in behaviour.

NLP is a wonderful behavioural engineering tool, an important breakthrough in the science of human communication. The term might sound long-winded but it really is quite simple. 'Neuro' refers to the brain; our sense of the outside world comes through our nervous system. 'Linguistic' refers to language, a system of communication; the way we perceive life is coded and transmitted through language. 'Programming' is the installation of a system or plan; all of our knowledge consists of a series of programmes that run our lives. NLP is the study of the effects of language, both verbal and non-verbal, on our nervous system. Your ability to do anything in life, from boiling an egg to making a million pounds, is directly related to the way you communicate with your nervous system. In other words, it is the study of how people do what they do. NLP is not an invention; it is a discovery. Neither is it a philosophy; it is a practical set of tools for acting effectively in the world. In a sense it is also an art, in that everyone who uses it does so through their own unique personality and style. The techiques of NLP will not teach you how to run your life, but if you know what you want to do, they can help you do it better.

NLP is a tool to understand and create human excellence in any form. You can use it to identify what it is that makes an individual person exceptionally skilled and acquire that skill for yourself in a fraction of the time. It is because we all share the same neurology that anything anyone else in the world can do, you can do too, simply by operating your nervous system in the same way. NLP is a way of automatically tapping in to the kind of experiences you want to have. Put simply, it is software for the brain.

In the way that a master chef has a recipe that consists of ingredients in certain quantities and a method to follow, all skilled masters, whether they be sports people, negotiators, salespeople or even hypnotists, have certain components to their work that can be learned simply by discovering their recipe, or strategy, for success.

All human behaviour comes from the use of our visual, auditory, kinaesthetic, gustatory and olfactory representation systems and our physiology. By improving that inner process, for example by copying the desirable aspects of successful people, we can improve our external performance. We all have our own strategies for motivation, love, confidence and happiness. We each have a certain process of inner events that we think and do to produce a particular quality of results.

Among Bandler and Grinder's original models of excellence were Milton Erickson, an extraordinary family therapist called Virginia Satir, the anthropologist Gregory Bateson and the founder of Gestalt therapy Fritz Perls. Bandler and Grinder observed the effective patterns of these people's behaviour, then coded and formatted them. They taught them to their students, who were able to apply them and achieve the same quality of results even though they did not have the therapists' years of experience. These were the patterns that formed the basis of NLP. Bandler himself describes it as 'an attitude (curiosity) and methodology that leaves behind a trail of techniques'.

They spent months video-taping and reviewing Erickson's work, deducing the components of his behaviour. John Grinder was accomplished at 'deep-trance identification', where he would put himself into an altered state and 'become' Erickson. He would move and speak as Erickson did and through this process unconsciously began to unravel many of the complexities of the master's words.

In addition to eliciting the strategies of these brilliant communicators, they found that all the highly effective people they studied generally operated out of a core of extremely useful presuppositions, or assumptions, about life, which ultimately form the basis of NLP. Whether these presuppositions are true or not is unimportant. By acting as though they are, a person who adopts them is in a more resourceful position. I recommend that you try operating from these assumptions if you don't already. Some of the most empowering ones are as follows:

1   There is no such thing as failure, only feedback. Every response is only information that can be used to tell you whether you are being effective or not.

2   People already have all the resources they need. All they need is access to these resources at appropriate times.

3   Anything can be accomplished if the task is broken down into small enough pieces.

4   People work perfectly; they are not broken. Everything they do is for a reason, even though the reason may seem inappropriate in some contexts.

5   The meaning of a communication is the response you elicit. Communication is *not* what you intend in what you say; it's about the response and experience you create in the listener.

6   The individual in any group with the most flexibility will also have control in that group.

NLP is, however, not just a series of beliefs; it is an organic tool in understanding the incredible complexities of the human being. Since it is impossible to look inside a person's brain to see how they accomplish something, instead Bandler and Grinder measured observable behaviour – body posture, breathing, facial expression, voice tonality – and from these observations made some fascinating discoveries.

First, they noticed that people tend to think predominantly in one of three sensory modes. Some people mainly make pictures in their imagination when thinking, others talk to themselves a lot of the time, while some go on their gut feeling.

1   VISUAL pictures
2   AUDITORY sounds
3   KINAESTHETIC touch, and occasionally gustatory/ olfactory – taste and smell

When you ask somebody, 'Do you remember playing as a child?' they might call to mind a *picture* of their school playground, hear the *sound* of children enjoying themselves, recall the *feeling* of running on a concrete surface and the excitement of a game, or the *taste* of sweets.

When people habitually use one system to the exclusion of others they become able to make greater distinctions in that sensory mode. No one system is necessarily any better than another, but certain contexts require certain kinds of thinking. A highly developed visual capacity is often a prerequisite of being a designer; many musicians can easily construct detailed sounds in their imagination; and footballers need to have well-developed kinaesthetic awareness, thinking with their body and particularly their feet. Highly effective people are able to use all systems, according to what they wish to accomplish.

## Eye-accessing Cues

Bandler and Grinder realized how important this information would be in creating better communication between people. They also deduced that the place someone moves their eyes to when thinking indicates which part of their nervous system they are accessing – that is, which sensory system a person is thinking in. From these signs, called eye-accessing cues, they could actually find out whether a person is predominantly visual, auditory or kinaesthetic. These cues are not a theory or philosophy; they are science.

When normally organized, right-handed people* are making pictures in their mind, they are accessing information from the visual system and their eyes move upwards – to their left to remember, to their right for constructed images. If they are listening to an internal sound, their eyes move to the side – once again to the left for remembered sounds and to the right for ones that are imagined. When they are involved in internal dialogue their eyes will be down to their left.

They further noticed that when someone is thinking predominantly in one system, their language indicates it.

| | |
|---|---|
| VISUAL | I *see* what you mean. |
| | I can *picture* that. |
| AUDITORY | It *sounds* good to me. |
| | That *rings* a bell. |

---

*The directions of eye movements may be reversed for left-handed people.

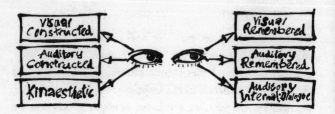

**Visual Constructed**

Seeing things in your mind that
you haven't seen before or
seeing things differently: e.g.
what would a pink dog
look like?

**Visual Remembered**

Seeing things that you have
seen before, as you saw them:
e.g. remember – is your front
door knob on the left or the right?

**Auditory Constructed**

Hearing sounds internally that
you have never heard before;
putting sounds and phrases
together in a new way: e.g.
what would your voice sound like
if it were deeper?

**Auditory Remembered**

Hearing sounds internally
that you have heard before:
e.g. what does your mother's
voice sound like?

**Kinaesthetic**

Feelings or emotions and
relating to touch: e.g.
what does snow feel like?

**Auditory Internal Dialogue**

Talking to yourself.

KINAESTHETIC    I'm glad you *touched* on that.
                He is a guy with a lot of
                *clout*.

They discovered that communication can be enhanced by talking to someone in the language they are thinking in. Remember that what we say is not as important as how we say it. You can determine an individual's system by watching his or her eye-accessing cues and by listening to the words being used. So if you're having a conversation with someone who is thinking in visual, then you'll create greater rapport by using visual words like 'clear', 'look', 'bright', 'imagine', 'show', 'envision', 'view'. If it's auditory, try 'listen', 'resonate', 'hear', 'attune'. For kinaesthetic, try 'grasp', 'feel', 'contact', 'touch', 'solid'.

Remember that NLP is not just a set of techniques; it is a curiosity that results in such. In the last few pages I have simply skimmed the surface. It may sound, look or even feel (depending upon the system you are using) like an advert for NLP, and in a sense it is. I frequently advise therapists or business people to take some NLP training. There are plenty of good courses, some of them in the UK and many more in the USA. For advice on NLP training you can write to me at PO Box 4RS.

NLP is only one of the many popular modern psychologies. These days there are any number of self-development concepts and technologies that involve or are derived from hypnotism – as the next chapter will show.

# 10

# The New Science of
# Personal Achievement

It is an incredible statistic that 80 per cent of all the information and technology that we have right now has been here only since 1964. More and more scientific and technological breakthroughs are taking place all around us at a breathtaking rate. We, as a human race, are connecting over greater and greater distances, exploring and reshaping the world around us. Calculations that used to take years, journeys that used to take months, are now made in hours. Evolution is unfolding and wherever it is we are going, we are going there fast.

Right now we live in an information age, with things like telephones, faxes, computers, and satellites all part of modern-day twentieth-century life. I believe that the next great stage in human development will be a move out of the information age and into a new time when people will begin to develop their inner resources: the age of psychotechnology, when we will begin to unleash the amazing powers and inner abilities with which we are all born. Right now most people put more effort into learning to work a video recorder than they do their own brain. For me the understanding and practice of hypnosis is like having an owner's manual for your brain.

Hypnosis is an excellent tool for self-development, self-programming and self-discovery. In my opinion 'traditional' positive thinking is not very effective. To create *real* change in an individual requires something more radical, a new self-image.

You may have heard of the idea that you are the sum total of your experiences, that everything that has ever happened to you has brought you to your personal here and now. More important than what has happened to you in life is the way you have *interpreted* your experiences. It is this representation that creates your self-image, what you think of yourself, and is essentially the blueprint for how you unconsciously create your life from moment to moment. Hypnosis is quite simply the quickest, easiest and most painless way of altering this blueprint, of changing your life.

It works a bit like a self-fulfilling prophecy: if you think of yourself as, say, unattractive, then unconsciously you will sabotage any attempts you make to try to appear attractive. If you truly believe you are unattractive, you won't represent yourself at your best and people will inevitably find you unattractive.

How you think of yourself also affects how other people feel about you, because they are constantly responding to your body language, tonality of voice and the emotional signals you are transmitting. All day long people are interpreting the congruency of your overall communication and the emotions that lay behind what you are saying. Remember that over 90 per cent of what we communicate is unconscious. You might be conveying one message with the words you use and another with your body language. By changing or re-presenting your self-image, you can not only like yourself more but *be liked more as well*.

Another important benefit of a strong self-image and sense of self is more relaxation, with consequent better health. One of the reasons for this is that, surprisingly, the nervous system cannot tell the difference between a physical threat to your life and a threat to your ego. Your mind reacts and triggers just the same chemical responses when your ego or values are threatened as it would if someone put a knife to your throat, although not to the same degree of intensity. However, if you think of how many times a day you feel threatened in little ways – someone cuts you up in traffic or your boss tells you off – you can begin to see the cumulative effect.

Sports people know the value of positive self-programming and many of them go through a mental rehearsal of their performance, which is a quasi-hypnotic process. An Arizona basketball team used this technique with incredible results. The coach sat one half of the team on the bench and told them to visualize throwing the balls into the basket, leaving the other half on the court throwing baskets for real. The players on the bench visualized shot after *successful* shot and the coach watched the tiny micro-muscular movements in their arms and fingers. They were actually establishing new neural pathways in their brains which created a successful shot link between their minds and their bodies. They were encoding successful shots into their kinaesthetic intelligence by repetition and through this technique radically improved as players.

There is even a new field of medical study known as psychoneuro-immunology, which deals with the interaction between the human mind and body. If you break the word down it is the inter-relationship of 'psychology' – your beliefs, values and self-perception – 'neurology' – your brain chemistry – and 'immunology' – your immune system. In other words, how you perceive yourself and the world affects your health.

Your possibilities at any moment in life are computed from your self-image. The better you think of yourself, the richer and more rewarding your life will be. This is not a new concept and is contained in every spiritual system of teaching on the planet.

In the early 1970s Maxwell Maltz, a plastic surgeon, wrote a best-selling book *Psycho-Cybernetics*. He noticed that altering the physical appearance of his patients through surgery often created a remarkable change in personality. However, it did not work with every single patient and some experienced no psychological benefits at all, no matter how spectacular the physical changes. Maltz concluded that cosmetic correction to the external appearance of a patient does not work when their internal self-image is poor or scarred. As Maltz says, 'We act, behave and feel according to what we consider this self-image to be and we do not deviate from this pattern.'

To show the effect of the self-image and how to change it, Maltz used cybernetics, a relatively new science that started in the 1940s that concerns control and communication in animals and machines. Living organisms and certain sophisticated machines have sensors that detect deviation from a set goal. They are able to feed back information which is interpreted so that corrections can be made to the output or behaviour of the organism or machine in order to keep it on target for the set goal.

The mind is rather like a heat-seeking missile, its goals or targets decided by unconscious programming, most of it done in the first six years of life. Your personality, your behaviour and life circumstances are a direct result of your self-image. Your self-image sets the boundaries of what you believe it is possible to achieve in life. Many people's self-image is so restrictive that they never really accomplish what they truly desire. One of the most effective ways to replace a negative self-image with a positive one is through hypnosis.

Two of the main factors that can cause negative self-image are resentment and guilt, both of which prevent people making a positive change to the way they perceive themselves.

A positive self-image of a responsible individual cannot exist in the mind of someone who is resentful – blaming others, society or fate for his or her lot in life. Taking responsibility for your life can often be enough to give you the power to change it. It works like this: if you take responsibility for your problems then you have the power to change them. By the way, responsibility is not the same as blame. If somebody comes to see me about a problem, I can tell pretty quickly whether they really want to get better or if they would rather just be right. Some people may well come along only to prove that hypnosis won't work, or that they are really messed up, or that their parents are at fault. It's hard to get somebody better without in the process showing them that they are responsible for themselves, and not everyone is ready to find that out.

The second cause of failure is guilt – feeling bad about something done in the past or even something that might be done in the future. The past and the future don't physically exist; they are there only in our heads. We cannot physically change the past or the future. If the only place the past and future exist is in your mind, through hypnosis you can change your mind.

This positive self-image 'theory' is the basis for a lot of modern self-help pop-psychology. As we enter this great new age of psychotechnology the self-development movement grows day by day. There are now thousands of books and tapes on the market that promise greater happiness, intelligence and enlightenment. It is wise to tread carefully through this maze of fantastic promises, but there are some treasures to be found. The books that I personally recommend are Anthony Robbins's *Unlimited Power*, Andrew Matthews's *Being Happy*, Maxwell Maltz's *Psycho-Cybernetics and Self-Fulfilment*, Napoleon Hill's *Think and Grow Rich*, Louise Hay's *You Can Heal Your Life* and Stuart Wilde's *Affirmations*.

None of these books is overtly about hypnosis but all of them deal with how to change your self-image. Of course, a positive self-image is not the answer to all of life's problems, but it will help you to interpret life differently, more resourcefully. It is another way of interpreting and undertanding human beings. I do not intend to try and explain away the amazing and multi-faceted aspects which make up the human psyche; my purpose is to give you a model through which you can interpret who you are. In the following pages I am going to show you how to programme yourself to become the person you would like to be. Vividly imagining success and happiness conditions your unconscious to make you think more positively. When you combine it with self-hypnosis, as I will show you, it leads to a better frame of mind and a richer, more fulfilled life. Remember, if you don't programme yourself then somebody else will – a religion, your peers, advertisers, etc.

## YOUR NEW SELF-IMAGE

### Who You Think You Are

The main filter for your perceptions is who you believe you are – your self-image – and that determines how you respond to the world. It controls your stress levels, your energy, your happiness, and everything about you.

During the 1950s the Koreans converted many American POWs to Communism. They didn't do it through torture or reward, but by changing the Americans' self-image. When you understand how they did it, you will see how your own self-image is formed and how you can change it to become the person you want. It will also come in pretty handy if you're ever captured by the Koreans!

The Koreans knew that behaviour is a direct result of

who we believe we are and that we are constantly confirming who we are by looking at our behaviour and the feedback we get from the outside world. In other words, there's a loop, and we need continual affirmation that we are who we think we are. The system to interpret our behaviour and feedback is our self-image. It's a Catch 22 situation.

So the Koreans interrupted the loop. Reprogramming men who had been highly trained to give only their name, rank and serial number was a big job, so they did it in small chunks at first. During an interrogation prisoners would be asked to make one or two anti-American or pro-Communist statements. For example, 'The United States is not perfect' or, 'In a Communist country unemployment is not a problem.' Once these apparently minor statements had been extracted, the prisoner would be asked to define exactly how the United States was not perfect. Worn down and weary, he would then be asked to sign his name to the list of reasons. Later he might have to read his list in a discussion group with other prisoners. He would be reading what he had said and signed himself.

The Koreans would then broadcast his name and list of

reasons during an anti-American radio programme, not only to his camp but to all the other North Korean POW camps and the American forces in South Korea as well. Suddenly he would find he had become a collaborator and even though it was unintentional, collaboration was defined as the kind of behaviour that helped the enemy.

When fellow prisoners asked why he had done it, he couldn't claim he had been tortured. He had to justify his actions in order to confirm his own internal sense of identity. He would say that what he said was true. In that moment his self-image changed. He now believed he was pro-Communist and his fellow prisoners reinforced his new identity by treating him differently.

Before long his new self-image would make him collaborate even more with the Koreans, so he could maintain his own integrity with who he believed he was. It had a snowballing effect. Psychological research has shown that human beings can only tolerate a certain amount of discrepancy between their thoughts and their behaviour. It's easy to be judgemental about the POWs, but if we look at ourselves and our own self-image, it is only the result of our childhood experiences, our parents' beliefs and values, peer pressure, religion and the media. The famous psychologist Eric Berne said, 'We are born princes and the civilizing process makes us frogs.'

The earliest messages you got from the world were from your family. Some of them were positive – 'You beautiful baby' – and some negative – 'You stupid boy/girl', 'Shame on you', 'Why are you always making a mess?' What's more, even when your parents love you, they don't always do exactly what you want. When you are very small they feed you, wash you and soothe you to sleep – it's like having two servants at your beck and call! Then, as you grow up, they know you have to learn to look after yourself, so they start asking you to do some of the work yourself. So you have to learn that being loved doesn't mean being spoilt! There is so much to take in.

When you are a little child so many people are bigger than you and seem to know more than you do. Then you start school and a whole new world of problems comes your way. Just as you're getting the hang of it, puberty arrives, hairs grow, the size of parts of your body changes and just being alive is highly embarrassing.

Through the media you are constantly exposed to people who appear to know exactly what is going on. The attractive, talented individuals who adorn the pages of magazines and star in TV programmes all have perfect skin and white teeth and are portrayed as happy and successful all day long.

All the time your self-image is being bombarded with messages that suggest somehow you are just not good enough. To reinforce that, there are those people around you with low self-esteem who covertly undermine you to make themselves feel better. Research has shown that by the age of fourteen 98 per cent of children have a negative self-image. They hate their bodies: they feel negative and insecure.[1]

Some people like to think they are completely different from their parents. I once worked with a man called Tom. His father was a priest and a staunch religious campaigner.

Due to his strict upbringing, Tom hated religion and deliberately campaigned against it. The irony was that he campaigned with all the style and fervour of a believer. He certainly knew how to influence people – just like his father! Whenever I looked at him I saw his father. Their beliefs may have been different but their values were the same.

Another example of how our self-image shapes us comes from social psychologist Steven J. Sherman, who conducted an amazing study. He wanted to see if he could increase the number of volunteers in a given area that would go door-to-door collecting for the American Cancer Society. He contacted a number of residents in the area by phone, explaining that he was doing a survey, and asked them to predict what they would say if asked to go door-to-door collecting for three hours. Of course, not wanting to seem uncharitable to the researcher or themselves, they said they would volunteer. As a result, because people had *committed* themselves during the survey, there was a 700 per cent increase in volunteers when an American Cancer Society representative called a few days later.[2]

As you can see, your self-image is a result of the decisions you have made about yourself. People will kill to protect their self-image, which is underpinned by their values. Therefore I believe it is important to know who you are. There are many ways in which we can define ourselves – 'I'm rich', 'I'm gentle', 'I am an entrepreneur', 'I'm black', 'I'm white', 'I am a shy person', 'I am outgoing', 'I am old', 'I'm a real man', 'I'm individual', 'I am careful', 'I'm the fastest', 'I don't care what people think of me', 'I'm

Catholic', 'I'm a Mercedes owner', 'I'm artistic', 'I'm practical', etc.

The places we go, the movies and television programmes we watch, the friends we have, the clothes we wear, the brands we buy, the car we drive, the job we do, our religion and many other things are a reflection of who we believe we are.

Take a moment right now to find out who you think you are.

First, get a piece of paper and brainstorm. Ask yourself, Who am I? How do I identify myself? If the ideas don't come at first, just write down some of the obvious things like your job, car, status, etc. Don't be too surprised by what comes up.

Next, close your eyes and get a clear, bright picture of yourself standing in front of you. Imagine that you don't know this person, think about him or her (do it with the same objective clarity you use for thinking about your friends). What kind of person is this in front of you?

Here are some questions that might help you:

- If you died tomorrow, who would be at your funeral?
- What kinds of things would be said about you?
- If you are honest with yourself, *what are your good points?* and *what are your bad points?*
- What is most important to your life?
- How would your mother/father describe you?
- What would your friends say about you behind your back?
- What would your enemies say about you?

Now score the following between 1 and 10 (1 being the lowest, 10 being the highest):

- How do you rate your physical appearance?
- How do you rate your personality?
- How do you rate your ability to create good relationships?
- How do you rate your appreciation of life?
- How do you rate your job satisfaction?
- How do you rate your creativity?

We all have infinite resources and possibilities, even though they may still be at an embryonic stage with us. Rather than attach yet another image or personality to yourself, allow your greater possibilities to come through. I personally believe that if there is a reason or purpose to life, this may be one of them: we are the universe's way of experiencing itself through our own personal infinite possibilities.

You can speed the process up and at the same time consciously take your life in a particular direction; you do not need to be at the mercy of your present life circumstances. When you have a good self-image it doesn't mean you don't have problems, because problems are how you learn and grow. Having a good self-image makes you more resourceful, so problems become challenges rather than obstacles.

In our culture there is a tendency to paper over the cracks of our unhappiness, believing that if only we have a bigger car, more jewellery, adoration, money, lovers, etc. it will somehow make us better. It may make us feel better temporarily, but it's like an addiction: once you start down that road you have to keep feeding the habit. Happiness is a *state*, not an achievement or goal. To put that another way, being happy is a way of doing something; you can't just be happy on its own – you are always doing something, even if it is just sitting still!

Of course it's great to have nice possessions and lots of money, but it is how you relate to those things that is important. I know millionaires who are constantly looking for their next million. If they could only stop for a moment and take a look around them, they would see how wealthy they really are.

I've had a man come to see me and say that what he wanted from life was money, so I asked him what money would do for him? He replied that it would give him security and freedom. He could see as well as I could that the real issue here was security and freedom, not money. So what we did was work on that, giving him the feelings of security and freedom that he needed. The way we did that was to use the simple self-image-change techniques that I am about to show you.

As you can see from that example, it is very important to be absolutely clear about what you really want from life. In order to have success with a self-image change, you must go to the values that underpin you. Otherwise you remain just a robot. You may indeed become a more successful robot with a bigger house, faster car and more money, but it is how you feel inside that is important.

Abraham Maslow, a psychologist who became famous in the 1960s, talked of man's 'hierarchy of needs'. He illustrated the concept as a pyramid. At the bottom of the pyramid are *physiological needs*, like survival. Above them come *safety needs*, which are security and protection. Then come *social needs*, belonging, acceptance and love, followed by *esteem needs*, status, prestige and acknowledgement. Finally, at the top come *self-actualizing needs*, which are personal fulfilment and growth. Maslow theorized that as each need is met you move up the pyramid until you make it to the magical place at the top of self-actualization.

Interestingly, he also thought that only unfulfilled needs motivate people. For example, if you are hungry you feel motivated to eat. If you need self-esteem you might try to impress your friends with a new car, stone-cladding for the front of your house, or spend a great deal of money on premium-branded products. It is the gap between what you think you don't have and what you think you want that provides the motivation.

However, let's look at this model from a different perspective and ask how self-actualized individuals get motivated to do anything. Are their lower needs being met because they have moved all the way up the pyramid? I think it is important to separate your higher values from external behaviours and possessions. You don't want to get stuck looking at the bottom of the pyramid; set your sights higher! For example, if you want a big house or a fast car, ask yourself what those things give you and then you will begin to get in touch with the values behind them that are important to you.

There is an excellent exercise, the Hexagon Exercise, devised by Michael Breen, that we frequently use in our seminars for getting people in touch with what they really want. It is about learning how to target the state that is connected with your higher values, so that once you learn to control your state you can start to work directly from your experience of fulfilment. Your efficiency is not impeded by having to prove yourself to someone (or to yourself), and you can see more clearly what really matters to you.

It's important to understand that goals and states are different. Goals or outcomes are related to certain behaviours or physical things in the world – they are *external*. States are *internal* and are the way you feel about something; and, as I have already said, that is under your control!

Many people tie their fulfilment to a particular outcome or a physical thing, such as money, sex, possessions, job, etc. However, if you target your values and achieve the inner state that supports them, you can start each day already feeling fulfilled. You then have a tremendous amount of energy and attention free to affect the external world and there is no longer any need to try to manipulate other people into giving you whatever it is that you thought you needed to feel good. You are now free to choose your goals for their inherent worth, not because you need to extract 'feeling good' from them. Do the Hexagon Exercise now and find out what it is that you *really* want.

## THE HEXAGON EXERCISE

1   Create a list of four goals, qualities or experiences that you would like to have or achieve.

   Write a few sentences about each one in the numbered lines in the right-hand column.

2   Create a code word or phrase that summarizes each of the goals.

   Write each code word in the rectangles next to the numbered lines.

3   Place the code word for each goal in the appropriately numbered hexagon on the left-hand side of the page.

4   Pair off the two goals on the top and the two on the bottom of the diagram.

5   For the paired goals at the top, vividly imagine, in detail, what it would be like to have achieved or fulfilled this pair of goals already. Then ask, 'Having achieved these two things, what does it do for me, get for me or give me?'

   Write down the answers in the blank hexagon that touches the top pair of goals.

6   For the pair of goals at the bottom, vividly imagine, in detail, what it would be like to have achieved or fulfilled this pair of goals already. Then ask, 'Having achieved these two things, what does it do for me, get for me or give me?'

Write down the answers in the blank hexagon that touches the bottom pair of goals.

7 Take the answers from steps 5 and 6, pair them together and ask again, 'If I had these two, what would they do for me, get for me or give me?'

Write down your answer in the connecting hexagon in the centre.

8 Now either go into a self-hypnotic state or simply vividly imagine what it's like to have the value or quality or goal that's written in the centre hexagon.

It's important to make the fantasy as real as possible. Think that it's happening right now.

9 Hold on to the sensations of this experience as you re-evaluate the four goals that you originally wrote down.

How does this affect your perception of the goals?

Does one goal become more important than the others?

Do one or more goals change?

Search for difference in how you feel about the goals having been through the process, etc.

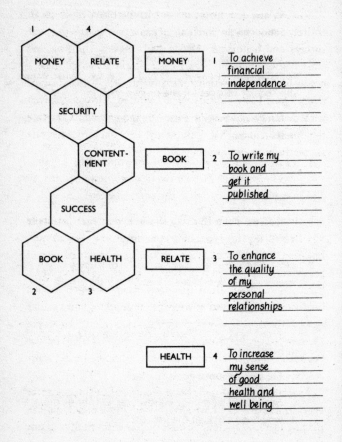

| | | |
|---|---|---|
| MONEY | 1 | To achieve financial independence |
| BOOK | 2 | To write my book and get it published |
| RELATE | 3 | To enhance the quality of my personal relationships |
| HEALTH | 4 | To increase my sense of good health and well being |

Exercise notes and diagram © *Michael Breen, 1991, 1993*

Success and happiness do not happen to people in an entirely random way. Each of us has a part in creating our success and happiness. After I had released the past and taken responsibility for who I was and who I wanted to be, I began to create a golden future for myself in my imagination. Once I knew inside what I wanted, I became driven with certainty and passion in the outside world. These are the fundamentals that I think are necessary to integrate successfully an empowering self-image.

### Releasing the Past

All of what we have learned to do at one time in some way helped us; it served, or serves, a purpose. Sometimes, however, although we have outgrown a particular pattern of behaviour, we keep on repeating it because it has become a habit. We may even think that habit is part of ourselves just because we are so used to having it around! As you create a new self-image, you will discover that a lot of what you thought was 'you' doesn't have to be 'you' at all. You can begin to choose to be more competent, more at ease, more responsible and responsive.

Resentments and unfinished emotional business can be very destructive, as I have already said, but it's no good just putting in a load of new, positive beliefs without first letting the old, inappropriate stuff go.

## EXERCISE ONE: RELEASING-THE-PAST TRANCE

Once you have relaxed into trance, imagine you are sitting in a cinema looking at the screen in front of you. Let an image appear on the screen of a time in the past when you felt some discomfort or unhappiness. Just remember that time and when you get to the point that you felt really bad, stop the movie. Now imagine getting up and stepping into the screen; step into the memory. Go over for a moment to the you in the film, the younger you from back then, and say whatever it is you need to comfort the younger you, to let him or her know it's going to be all right. They didn't know it at the time, but you survived that experience. Let that younger you know that they turn out to be stronger than they thought, and that they have got a friend in you. You may even want to embrace them or give them a cuddle. When you have done that, step back out of the picture and shrink the screen until it's tiny. Drain out all the colour so all you can see now is a tiny black-and-white photograph of something you survived in the past and then just float off into the distance.

I recommend finding a handful of incidents from the past and doing the preceding trance exercise with them. One per day is enough.

## EXERCISE TWO

Once you have relaxed into trance, imagine you are sitting in your cinema again, looking at the screen in front of you. Let an image appear on the screen of someone you feel resentment towards. Now tell that person exactly how you feel about them; say whatever it is you need to say in order to heal the way between you. Remember, you don't have to like someone in order to forgive them. You don't have to trust them; you just have to let them go. See the tie of resentment like a rope connecting you and that person. Now take a pair of scissors and cut the rope, letting them and the resentment go. Once again you can make the screen with them on it black and white, drain out all the colour, shrink the screen and spin it off into space. Have some fun if you like and shrink and send off that image in your own way. A golfer I worked with shrank all his negative images into golfballs and hit them with a magnificent shot way off over the horizon.

I have found it very useful in the past to think of the way that great men have been able to rise above their difficulties, and see disaster and defeat with compassion and equanimity. One of the greatest men of this century, Mahatma Gandhi, in his dying moments, turned to his assassin and made the Hindu sign for forgiveness.

You can use this exercise as often as you need to.


EXERCISE THREE

As soon as you have relaxed into trance, find yourself sitting in your cinema again. Let a time of discomfort or unhappiness come to mind and see it on the screen like a movie. While it is taking place, stop the film again. Now go back to just before the event and imagine what would have happened if it had never occurred. Run through the events that would have followed. How would your life have been different? What experiences would you not have had? Ask yourself what this unhappy event gave you. What did you learn and what did it do for you? When you have finished looking at your alternative history, go back and reinsert the uncomfortable incident in the time and place it occurred on the screen. Shrink it and spin it off into the distance, or imagine it behind you.

The great thing about this particular exercise is that it gives you the opportunity to look at things in different ways. Without doing this we have only the sequence of events and our judgements of them that were recorded in our minds at the time.

We all have the equivalent of a state-of-the-art video- and audio-recording studio inside our heads. Why not use it to give us more useful perspectives on life?

You may remember how I emphasized earlier in the section 'Neuro-Linguistic Programming' (page 154–161) that the most powerful individual in the group is always the most flexible. The more perspectives you have, the more flexible you are.


## CREATING A NEW SELF-IMAGE

Although I consider myself an enthusiastic and confident person, the truth is I wasn't born feeling this way. It was only a few years ago that I learned how to run my brain more efficiently to increase my confidence. I decide to feel confident by imagining how good I will feel when I have done whatever it is I am setting out to do, and I amplify that feeling to give me an inner sense of certainty that drives me to become competent. It helps to look forward to, to *anticipate*, the pleasure of competence while you are still learning. The learning is faster, and more enjoyable.

Here are some ways to establish your new self-image. It can be a total self-image change, impinging on all areas of your life, or just a partial one – for example, being a better golfer, public speaker or negotiator.

## EXERCISE ONE: A PERFECT PLACE

When you have relaxed into trance, take yourself to a time when everything is all right, is exactly as it should be. Notice where are you and what you are aware of, notice everything you can, making finer and finer sensory distinctions which will enrich the experience.

For example, when I am working with someone who finds themselves in their dream home I ask them to tell me what colour the wallpaper is, how the floor feels, etc. We move through the house, looking at each room, finding validation of their success and happiness.

Once when I was doing this same exercise with a writer, on the bookshelf she saw leather-bound copies of the books she was going to write. On the desk there was a family photo, and as we moved into the living room the children she hoped to have were there and she felt the joy of embracing them.

For a businessman, he might find himself in a big stylish office and enjoy the feelings of achievement that the awards or sales figures displayed around his office give him, the beautiful view from his window, the friendly respectful staff who enter his office for meetings.

The finer the sensory descriptions you can make about the experience the better. So, for example, at first you might see a picture on the wall; as you move closer you can notice the details of it and if you take it off the wall there may be something written on the back. All the time that you are enjoying the experience of your future success, you are encoding that experience into your brain. You are telling your unconscious, 'I want more of this, please.' By focusing on happiness, by rehearsing your success over and over again, you create new neural pathways in the brain; you are programming yourself for success.

The way I like to finish this exercise is by noticing where I feel the nicest feelings most strongly in my body. Then I imagine that those feelings are a certain colour. Then I move that colour or aura slowly around my body, taking the feeling with it. When the colour is glowing all around my body, I imagine turning up the brightness and intensity of the colour. Of course, the feelings follow, so I turn the colour up even more, until it fills the whole room. When I've done that, I imagine the colour spreading out of the room, gradually picking up speed as it races out, faster and faster, until it covers the whole of the world. Then I feel it racing back to me, and with a woosh it impacts back into my body. I usually float in that beautiful feeling before awakening.

Do this every day for three weeks. After twenty-one days, you will find that it has encoded itself definitively in you. As I've said, all successful actors, sales people, musicians and sports people use some form of mental rehearsal; this is the 'turbo' version.

## EXERCISE TWO: SETTING AN OUTCOME

I believe that in life you get back whatever you put out. So if you are unclear and fuzzy about what you want, that is what you will get back from life. Like anything, it takes practice; the more you focus on exactly what you want, the more likely you are to get it. It's a good idea to allow yourself to fantasize and dream, but do it with the focus of a laser beam. It is also helpful to have an evidence procedure – in other words, ask yourself how will you know when you have achieved the outcome you desire.

Once you have relaxed into trance, focus on one of your goals. What will it be like when you have achieved it? Fully immerse yourself in the experience. Notice what you are seeing, hearing, feeling, smelling and tasting. Allow the experience to encode into every cell of your brain like water soaking into a sponge. The richer your sensory experience of your goal the better. If your goal is to have a sports car, imagine what it will look like, how the engine will sound and the seats feel; will you be able to smell the leather interior?

If your goal is a relationship, you may find it better to focus upon sensory information that you will experience in the context of the relationship than try to make a picture of your perfect partner.

Once you are in a trance, ask yourself how you will feel

when you are in a perfect harmonious relationship. What will it feel like to enjoy special moments of intimacy? Some people like to be told that they are loved, so simply imagine your perfect partner saying those things to you that make you feel loved. Some people need to be touched in a certain way; others like to be brought presents to feel loved. Use whatever works best for you.

### EXERCISE THREE: YOUR IDEAL LIFESTYLE

Once you have relaxed into trance fantasize about your ideal lifestyle. Imagine your perfect day, the places you go, the kind of people you meet, the things you do, the way you are treated. Really focus on every detail in your experience of your ideal. What do you have for breakfast? How do you get to work? What do you do? How do you feel at the end of your perfect day? Whether you imagine receiving the gift of a diamond ring or being held and gently kissed or just told that you are loved, run it through in your mind. Amplify the experience by making the voice louder, or the image of the ring really big and bright; bring it closer and send a strong message to your unconscious mind of what you want. Remember, your nervous system cannot tell the difference between a real and an imagined experience, so this fantasized rehearsal prepares you and orients you towards your goals.

A good way of generating new and exciting ideas about what you want from life is to ask yourself, 'What would I do if I knew I couldn't fail?'

If you stop and look at the world around you for a

moment, not the earth but the world which is man-made, most of what you see started as a thought in someone's head. Even you and I did. The power of creative thinking is immense, because before something can happen in the external world it must first happen in the internal world.

The wonderful things about hypnosis and trance is that you can go anywhere, do anything, be anyone. You can create an ideal reality in the privacy of your own mind. Play with it until you get it just right.

It is also worth doing an 'ecology' check – that is, run through your ideas to see that your outcomes ultimately support you and your environment. It's no good having the goal of achieving wealth at the cost of your health or the safety of others. It is also worth remembering to pace yourself – you don't want to work so hard for your millions that you don't see your family until you are immensely rich and you meet your wife again in the divorce courts! Enjoy your voyage to success, and take it easy from time to time.

EXERCISE FOUR: WHO WILL YOU HAVE TO BECOME?

In order to have the things you want and do the things you want to do, you need to ask yourself who you will have to become. This is where the real shift in self-image begins to occur. One of the things I immediately noticed when I was fantasizing my ideal lifestyle was that I would have to change some of the aspects of myself.

Ask yourself what kind of person has the lifestyle that you want. How do they dress, speak and move? What do they know and who do they know and what is important to them? What do they smile at and what do they stand for?

## EXERCISE FIVE: GOAL-SETTING

When you've relaxed into trance, make a clear, bright picture that represents the sum total of all the previous exercises. A picture that encompasses the new you and your ideal lifestyle. One man I worked with imagined himself with a beautiful wife and kids all looking healthy with big smiles on their faces. They were standing outside a huge mansion with a Rolls-Royce parked in the driveway. He told me that inside the house were some of the successful books he had written and some videos of his TV shows. In his desk were bank statements showing huge sums in credit. This image contained a symbol for everything he wanted.

Whatever you imagine, remember it has no meaning except the meaning you give. As soon as you have the picture that represents what you want, decide how long it will take you to achieve it. Maybe a year, two years or five years. Then, working back from your outcome, figure out the steps that took you to your goal. Make pictures that represent the milestones, the major steps on the way, get smaller and smaller until you get all the way back to where you are now.

The important thing about time is that we sort it in our own unique way. Try an experiment now. Stop a moment and pick an everyday behaviour you have done in the past, do now and will do again in the future; like cleaning your teeth. First, think about doing it a year ago, then doing it

now, and finally doing it a year in the future. Where in your personal space do you hold the images of those three events? For me the past is behind me, the present is located approximately two inches in front of my face and the future runs like a track out in front of me, angled to the right. However, some people sort time all out in front of them with the past on the left, the future on the right. Rather like looking at a strip of movie film. Find out how yours are, then slot in big, bright pictures of the events that you would like to have happen in your future. For example, the man with the big house and family had five steps. Step four was the big deal he clinched that enabled him to buy the house. Step three was his children being born. Step two was sudden opportunity in his professional life. Step one was sending out information, his portfolio and his prospective ideas, to people who might be able to help him.

Some people do this sort of thing all the time, but often it is automatic, unplanned and unstructured. Thinking like this really does make you master of your own destiny.

Of course, all this planning is futile if you don't take action. Some people sit around and day-dream without ever doing a thing. However, by creating a vivid representation of how you ideally want to live your life and focusing on it every day, you will be motivated to take action and you will know where you are going. Fantasize, rehearse, then go out into the world and *do it*! Start with step one, *today*. As General Paton said, 'A good plan violently executed right now is far better than a perfect plan executed next week.'

# 11

# Everyday Hypnosis

## ADVERTISING

Every second of every minute of every day our consciousness is bombarded with millions of messages of sensory
awareness. Some of these are messages from friends and
relations; some are from advertisers, politicians, the media
and religious groups. From every area of our world,
messages pervade our consciousness and shape who we are.
Most people are asleep to this everyday hypnosis.

I often hear people say that advertising has no effect on
them. We all like to think that we are in charge of our
own decisions. However, the people who decide to spend
hundreds of millions of pounds on advertising every year
aren't just trying to get rid of their money. Their research
tells them that a well-structured campaign will deliver the
message they want to the public. Of course, no advertising
can guarantee to affect a specific individual, nor does it all
work all the time. As Lord Leverhulme said, 'Half the
money I spend on advertising is wasted. I just don't know
which half.'

Think how different the world would be without

advertising. There would be no commercials, just a list of new products available each month.

Surely it's not a coincidence that supermarkets are such hypnotic environments – the fluorescent lights, the inane background music tinkling away and the colourful product packaging blaring out at you. All these things alter your consciousness and put you in a more suggestible state. I am always seeing people in a supermarket trance, with a can of beans in one hand and a can of peas in the other, looking into space. Just the other day I was in a supermarket buying some beer. I picked up the supermarket's own brand and at that moment saw a well-advertised brand sitting on the shelf in front of me. Suddenly I didn't feel as good about the beers I had in my basket and actually felt better when I swapped them over for the well-advertised brand. It was only at that point that I realized how I had been influenced.

Probably one of the biggest misconceptions about advertising is that it is only peripheral. People have the television or radio on but because it is in the background believe they are not being influenced. That, however, is exactly why advertising is so powerful. The messages of the commercials are going into your mind at a pre-conscious level and through repetition they are effective.

Advertisers understand that what influences us is not our intellect but the sensations we link to their products. The main way in which advertising works is through *association*. In the early years of the twentieth century the Russian scientist Ivan Pavlov was conducting conditioned-response experiments. The most famous of these involved offering some food to one of his dogs and at the same time ringing a bell. After he had done this several times the dog associated the bell with food and within a short while Pavlov would only have to ring the bell for the dog to salivate.

Pepsi have realized the power of association with pop stars like Michael Jackson, Lionel Richie, MC Hammer and Tina Turner. Many people have experienced good feelings listening or dancing to their music, so by advertising the product alongside the music good feelings are associated with the product. For example, Lionel Richie will sing one of his love songs, evoking good feelings while Pepsi flashes on the screen. In future, when people think of Pepsi they will feel good.

Rather than being associated with an individual, some drinks are sold on the back of a lifestyle. Martini drinkers are portrayed as young, rich, jet-setting, stylish, smiling individuals with not a care in the world. If you stop to think about it, though, being young, rich and stylish has nothing at all to do with your alcohol intake.

Advertisers know that many of our decisions are unconscious, emotional responses to our environment, not carefully contemplated and logical moves. They appeal to our emotions and are expert at generating states and linking ideas to them. At the time of writing, there is an advertisement for Volkswagen that goes straight to the point and makes the association overtly. The commercial is a series of sound-bites of 'everyday' people speaking and the dialogue runs as follows:

'It's like having ten yards of that plastic bubble stuff to pop, all on your own. It's like waking up at half seven thinking it's Monday and then realizing it's actually Sunday. It's like when you're going through your jeans and you're about to put them into the washing machine and you find a tenner that you wasn't expecting. It's like when you're round at a friend's house for dinner and they say please have some more, it'll only go to waste. It's like being half-way down a really long supermarket queue and then seeing them opening a checkout next to you and getting there first. Driving the new Volkswagen Golf, however, you choose to describe it as one of life's true pleasures'.

This has been scripted to remind those listening of their own personal pleasures and then links them to the Volkswagen.

By continued exposure to a commercial, new neural pathways are formed. As Jack Trout, the American marketing guru, has observed, the mind is where the ultimate marketing war takes place – the battles between brands are fought not in the shopping malls but in your mind.

The brain is a mass of millions of neural pathways with each idea or memory moving along its own. Whenever we experience intensity our brain encodes a memory of the sequence of behaviour that leads to it in our nervous system. If the experience is intensely unpleasant, we learn to avoid the events that lead to it. This is an extremely efficient system. For example, if a baby sticks its hand on something hot it gets a sensation of pain and so knows not to do that again.

Whenever we do something new we create a neural pathway, so that we can reaccess that experience again easily. Each time we repeat a particular behaviour we strengthen the neural pathway. Research has shown that neural pathways in the brain get physically bigger through repetition of behaviour. That is how people become 'hard-wired' to certain automatic behaviour like smoking and over-eating.

The idea that it takes twenty-one days to create a habit has a lot of truth in it. However, if an experience is of enough emotional intensity it can take just one day. Some people are amazed that others cannot see through these illogical associations. However, Dr Cialdini, the famous researcher in social influence, says, 'The important thing for the advertiser is to establish the connection. It doesn't have to be a logical one, just a positive one.'

In one study men who saw a new car advertisement that included a seductive young woman model rated the car as faster, more appealing, more expensive-looking and better designed than men who viewed the same ad without the model. Yet when questioned later, the men refused to believe that the presence of a model had influenced their judgement.[1]

With the recent interest in environmental and health issues, many advertisers have labelled their products 'natural'. However, when you stop to think about it, the idea is ridiculous because everything is natural – a nuclear bomb uses natural nuclear energy, but just one could really ruin your day!

At the time of writing there is also a very effective TV campaign to encourage viewers to drink more milk, featuring a milkman talking to dancing milk bottles. From the beginning the advert takes you to an unreal world and obvious associations with Disney-like cartoons and fantasy films of childhood, which act as an excellent regression to remind viewers of fun times when they were children. The ad finishes with the great line, 'Your milkman can deliver all the milk you'll ever need.' First, this presupposes you need milk, but more importantly, who else delivered the milk you needed as a child? Your mother did! A very basic, but incredibly powerful appeal is made with just that one line.

## THE NEWS MEDIA

The cultural hypnosis we are all subject to extends much further than advertising. Even if the only programme you watch on your television is the news, you are still being influenced. Every day we listen to the radio, watch television and read papers, but is the news *really* what is going on?

For example, some of the people who come to see me with a fear of flying have had that fear instilled in them more or less directly by the media. All of them had vivid recollections of repeated stories of air crashes; one man had even seen news footage of wreckage and bodies as a child. If we look at the facts, driving a car is actually twenty-five times more dangerous than flying, but these same people were not scared of travelling in a car. Statistically you are more likely to be kicked to death by a donkey than die in an air crash. Now, I've had some strange cases over the years, but none of them dealt with an inexplicable fear of donkeys!

The media loves disasters and the more sensational they are the better. Our news bulletins are packed with stories of personal tragedies and crimes, and hardly a night goes by without a crime programme re-enacting some gruesome felony or docu-drama reliving it as entertainment.

If the news were reported in an unsensational way, with a more balanced perspective, it would go something like this: 'Today millions of people got up and went to work. Tragically, thirty of them died in an air crash.' However, just like advertising, news reporting is a business and owners have papers to sell, TV companies have ratings to achieve. Truth is not as important as sensation. Unfortunately, the way that the news is represented leaves a lot of people feeling frightened and unsafe, which then makes them suspicious, untrusting and even unhappy. We don't even know why it is we feel this way, but it is not really surprising when we are served up a daily dose of terror and misfortune.

Even more worrying is the huge increase in popularity of violent action films. While they excite the audience, they also promote a powerful message that violence is the way to get things done. There have been numerous studies on the effects of these violent films on the public. One of the ways psychologists evaluate these films is to show one to a group of children and then watch them play for a couple of hours afterwards to see if it makes a difference. Of course, it doesn't make any immediate difference, but exposure to the media has a cumulative effect over a certain period. If you look at the rise in violent crime since, for example, the 1980s, there is your evidence.

## LANGUAGE

In one sense people are in a profound trance all day long – the trance is called language. Historically, as language developed, rational and logical thinking came to dominate and words became a way of labelling our experience. However, language can never do justice to the speed of our thinking or the complexity and senstivity of our experience; it can only be an approximation. In other words, the map is not the territory and the menu is not the food!

Language is a filter for our perceptions. It is a massive cultural agreement and shapes the way we experience the world. The Eskimos have names for seventy different kinds of snow, because in order to survive they have to make such very fine distinctions. These distinctions are unimportant, and therefore practically meaningless, to people who see snow only a few times a year.

If there is no word or representation of something in your brain's vocabulary for an experience, it is very hard to include it into your world. When Captain Cook first landed in New Zealand the natives who were there fishing paid no attention to his big ship nearby, because it was so far outside of their range of concepts that to them it was invisible. When he landed they could see him and his crew but could not see the ship he had sailed in. This idea sets up all kinds of trains of thought. Some people believe that we are visited by angels or extraterrestrials, but most do not have the perceptual concepts to be aware of them. Some people who see my stage show for the first time have to declare it fake and the participants actors, because they do not have a framework for understanding stage hypnosis and they do have one for actors and trickery.

The power of language shapes our perception of life in other ways as well. Although words are one of our tools of communication, they are inherently meaningless. We give words their meaning by the associations we make with them. While we can all agree on the meaning of words like apple or house, it is much more difficult to get all-round agreement on what love, freedom, justice or guilt are. That's because they are concepts created by humans, with many shades and distinctions.

Words are essentially triggers or associations for certain experiences, and everyone's experience is unique. Successful communicators artfully use the strengths and weaknesses of language. Some of them speak in a way that is ambiguous or vague enough to enable others to create the meaning they desire. Politicians are masters at eloquently talking rubbish and making it sound as though they are saying something meaningful. They are experts at never directly answering questions, and can talk on and on sincerely about absolutely nothing, leaving the listener to create a meaning.

When a friend of mine who is a hypnotherapist was placing newspaper ads offering his services, rather than list all the numerous problems people could come to him with – smoking, slimming, phobias, eczema etc. – he simply put:

**SORT IT OUT**
with Hypnotherapy

This invited the reader to find out whatever 'it' meant for

them and give the ad the meaning that was specific to them. Needless to say, the approach was very effective.

This technique can be used less honourably. Newspaper astrologers, fake 'psychics', 'channellers' and 'mediums', and dubious cult leaders all use the ambiguity of language to make it appear that they are saying a great deal more than they are committing themselves to. Consider this, which I picked out at random from my daily paper:

*Taurus*: The frustration of your present situation is that there is still so much you could achieve if only you had the time and energy to spare. The answer is simplicity itself – stop doing what others want you to do and start doing only what suits you.

This little paragraph could apply to, let us say, 90 per cent of the population 90 per cent of the time. Who doesn't wish for a bit more time and energy? Who doesn't feel imposed upon by the wants and demands of others, and feel that if only they could do what they wanted things would be better? The seer can hardly go far wrong with this, having offered no description whatsoever of *what* the present situation is, *what* you could achieve and *what* others want you to do.

I witnessed a demonstration recently where the 'psychic' said he was getting a message from 'A John, a Jane, a Jimmy or a Jeff'. He asked, 'Why do I see a uniform?' The vagueness of the name meant that any name beginning with 'J' would be picked up. The uniform could have been anything from a cavalry officer's to a traffic warden's, and the grateful recipient of the message was happy to offer a friend or relative of the deceased to fill it. And so it went on. Each time he offered a non-specific reference, the entire audience searched their minds to find someone who might fit the broad description offered. The believer might wonder, of course, why it is that these obliging and communicative spirits are so vague with their names – does death not destroy us but just give us dyslexia?

Of course, there are positive sides to astrology and many psychic phenomena, and there is certainly more to heaven and earth than science yet knows of, but knowledge of hypnotic language patterns can stop us from reading too much into what has not yet been proved.

*Good* sales people instinctively use language to create the experience of owning the product or having the service in the mind of the buyer, so that they can decide whether to have it or not. 'Imagine how good you will look, how relaxed you will feel, how fast you can go, driving this car, sir.'

Honest sales people don't try to coerce people to buy things; but they help them to make the correct decision by giving them a sensory rich experience. 'Years from now you will look back and feel glad that you saved money and made your life easier by investing in *x*.' Although this form of selling can, like anything, be abused, some sales people create unrealistic experiences in the minds of buyers, concentrating upon the positive aspects and ignoring the negatives. Politicians, lawyers and many other professionals do this as part of their jobs.

I frequently witness the distortions in everyday language that create problems when somebody says one thing but means another. Parents can easily hypnotize their children into certain types of behaviour unconsciously through the language they use. For example, a mother who snaps at her child, 'Why do you *always misbehave*' is implying to the child that its behaviour is permanent, and in this way she is embedding a command that is likely to produce bad behaviour.

Early in our education we are taught to use what linguists call nominalizations – that is, changing a verb (a doing or process word) into a noun (a static thing). For example, in saying you cannot handle a relationship, you are talking about a relationship as if it were a static physical thing, like a teapot, rather than talking about relating – a dynamic, active process of communication. The problem arises because the art of relating, when it is referred to as a relationship, is perceived as static and no responsibility is being taken for the active, continuing process of relating with another person. When someone systematically nominalizes, they can restrict the amount of choices they have because they perceive the world in a more static and fixed way.

Never underestimate the power of words. They can put us in good moods or bad moods and even, in extreme cases, start wars.*

Another very hypnotic experience is going to church. There is the cross to fixate upon, and then the repetition of

*For a more detailed understanding of how language shapes our thinking, I recommend you read about the NLP meta-model and Milton model in *Structure of Magic*, Vol. 1, and *Patterns of Hypnotic Teachings of Milton Erickson*, Vol. 1.

prayers and closing your eyes, and in some cases the personal magnetism of the priest or vicar can carry you away. Many of the American TV evangelists are really effective hypnotists. Listen to the content of what they are saying. 'Close your eyes and let the Lord come into your life' is very similar in structure as my telling hypnotic subjects on the stage to close their eyes and let relaxation come into their bodies.

In the way that American bartenders put a few dollar bills in their tip jars at the beginning of the evening to give the impression that tipping with folding money is the norm, church ushers do the same with their collection baskets. A research team at Arizona University infiltrated the Billy Graham organization and reported on similar advance preparations. 'By the time Graham arrives in town and makes his altar call, an army of six thousand waits with instructions on when to come forth at varying intervals to create the impression of a spontaneous mass outpouring.'[2]

A further example of everyday hypnotic subjects are soldiers, because army training is largely a process of breaking down the critical faculty, the ability to question and analyse. Marching is a good example of unquestioned response to a suggestion. This creates a pattern of behaviour in the soldier, so in future when an order is given he automatically responds. An army would be ineffective if every man stopped to consider the rights and wrongs of each of his actions. You can probably imagine the response to a soldier questioning an instruction. 'You're not here to think, lad, you're here to obey orders!'

While anaesthetized, patients are sensitive to the things

said within their environment. Bandler and Grinder talk about a patient whose behaviour became self-destructive following an operation. The surgeon had said, 'It looks terrible, I don't think she's going to make it for very long.' This statement acted as a hypnotic suggestion because the patient was in a suggestible state. Luckily this was realized in time and rectified.[3]

One of the main reasons I advocate using self-hypnosis is because, as I have already said, if you don't take responsibility for programming yourself, then someone else will. Advertisers, religious leaders, politicians, your peers and numerous other sources are all bombarding your sensory awareness all day long with their messages. As you become more aware of the messages that impinge on your consciousness, you can make more informed choices about what sort of television programmes to watch, and laugh at how the advertising people and religious organizations are doing their best to try and influence you.

You, and only you, have the power to de-hypnotize yourself from this everyday cultural hypnosis, simply by becoming aware of it and bringing it to your conscious attention.

# 12

# Dangers and Abuses of Hypnosis

## MIND CONTROL

How was it that apparently ordinary people became involved in acts of mass murder following Hitler's rise to power in Germany in the 1930s and 1940s? A psychologist named Stanley Milgram tested people for obedience to authority and found that over 90 per cent of his students would obey orders, even if they believed that doing so caused physical suffering to others. He says, 'The essence of obedience consists in the fact that a person comes to view himself as the instrument for carrying out another person's wishes and therefore no longer regards himself as responsible for his own actions.'[1]

I have been asked on more than one occasion if Hitler was a hypnotist. If I am to answer the question honestly, I would have to say no. Hitler used manipulation, coercion and trickery to encite people to do evil things; hypnosis on its own is not a sufficient tool to accomplish what he did. He was influenced along with many others, including Freud, on the subject of crowd psychology by a writer called Gustav Le Bon, who made some fascinating observations, including the following:

> Whoever the individuals that compromise it [a crowd], however like or unlike be their mode of life, their occupations, their character, or their intelligence, the fact that they have been transformed into a crowd puts them in possession of a sort of collective mind which makes them feel, think and act in a manner quite different from that in which each individual of them would feel, think and act were he in a state of isolation. . . The most careful observations seem to prove that an individual submerged for some length of time in a crowd in action soon finds himself . . . in consequence of the magnetic influence given out by the crowd of which we are ignorant in a special state which much resembles the state of fascination in which the hypnotized individual finds himself in the hands of the hypnotizer.[2]

The Nuremberg rallies are explicit examples of Hitler's calculating manner of manipulation of the mind. Everything about them – the colours, the use of spotlights, the placement of the spectators, the chanting of the mantra '*Sieg Heil*' and the focus upon the Führer – was carefully plotted. He would skilfully build his rhetoric to a climax and lead the crowd into a frenzy. In this altered state of consciousness the masses became very suggestible and ultimately influenced.

However, let's not ignore the striking similarity to the rock concerts of today, where often a positive sense of mass hysteria is experienced.

Acts of mass influence, though, are not limited to stadiums. Interestingly, Serge Moscovici, in his book *The Age of the Crowd*,[3] says that these days we 'have leaders who, in their newspaper offices or in front of their radio microphones or television cameras, mesmerize a thousand times as many individuals as their predecessors'.

One of the main areas where mind control is alive and kicking is among many of today's spiritual groups and cults. During a meditation session, which is a consciousness-altering process, a cult member may receive suggestions that mould him or her to the cult's doctrine. Disruption of eating and sleeping patterns, restricted contact with the outside world, repetition, forced attention and hyperventilation are disorientation tactics which alter awareness and reduce a person's critical faculties. Then irrational beliefs can be implanted, such as 'The outside world is the arena of falsehoods' or, 'The cult is made of chosen people who have to save the world.'

Many of today's cults practise mind control in a social context. Individuals are immersed in a social environment where they must let go of their old identity and assume the new one of the group. The process can take place within a few hours and then a few days later will be established. The fundamental essence of mind control is to encourage dependence, conformity and devotion and discourage individuality and personal freedom.

## HYPNOSIS AND CRIME

There should really be no need for (and no content to) this section, as there is no greater link between hypnosis and crime than there is between hypnosis and potatoes. However, as long ago as 1894 a book was published that associated the two in the public mind. The book was actually a work of fiction, *Trilby*, by George du Maurier, about a young artist's model and her affair with a painter. A minor character, but one important for the plot, is Svengali, who hypnotizes the heroine, Trilby, to cure her headache and later hypnotizes her again to seduce her and train her to sing on stage. The character caught the public imagination and his name became a byword for a person with dubious mesmeric influence.

However, although there is no link between hypnosis and crime, there is a link between power and abuse. Fairly regularly a psychotherapist or a doctor is prosecuted for abusing their patients. As we went to press a hypnotherapist in Essex was being investigated under suspicion of having molested his clients.

There have been other similar cases in recent years. In 1988 Michael Gill was gaoled for two years at Caernarvon Crown Court for assaulting women, having first allegedly put them into a trance using a flashing light. In 1991 Nelson Nelson was jailed for eleven years for abusing more than 100 girls, again after using hypnosis.

In Holland Leo Vachta raped eighty women at his practice in Amsterdam. He was jailed for eighteen months in 1989 for having sex with 'persons deprived of willpower'.

These cases are all an appalling betrayal of a supposedly therapeutic relationship. But what part did the hypnosis play? During the same period countless therapists and doctors who did not use hypnosis abused their patients, and we know only of the ones who got caught! In a recent survey a large number – some $7\frac{1}{2}$ per cent – of American psychotherapists admitted to having had an affair with a client.

Jeffrey Masson's book *Against Therapy*[4] recounts in graphic detail some of the more heinous examples of this sort of abuse.

If you are visiting a hypnotherapist for the first time I would suggest that you take three simple precautions:

1  Try to visit a therapist who has been personally recommended to you. If this is not possible, then ask the therapist for names of previous clients who would recommend him or her.

2  Take a friend with you to the session to make sure that you are not alone.

3  Lastly, if you feel at all uneasy with the therapist, then simply find another one – there are plenty to choose from! If you are a woman, you may prefer to see a female therapist.

These precautions are sensible, but at the same time I have to maintain what I have already stated – that by using hypnosis *alone* you cannot get people to do things that are in conflict with their morals and values. However, you certainly can through manipulation, coercion or trickery. André Weitzenhoffer, who has researched and published on hypnosis for over forty years, has stated that he believes it is possible to make a subject commit a criminal or antisocial act only 'when the subject does not perceive the situation as being antisocial'.[5]

Apart from cases of therapists who happen to be hypnotists molesting patients, there have also been some sensational incidents of people apparently being programmed to commit criminal acts without their knowledge.

When examining this area we must not forget that there are people who choose to commit criminal acts. They deliberately break the law and, when they are caught, they certainly don't all suddenly become law-abiding. Many will lie and cheat and blame others in order to escape bearing the responsibility for their own actions. Blaming a hypnotist may be corny, but that doesn't stop people trying it on.

Faced with evidence from laboratory experiments that seemed to indicate that hypnotic subjects would commit crimes if ordered to do so, Milton Erickson conducted some experiments of his own to see if the results were really valid.

He knew that a subject in a hypnotic trance would understand the context in which they were hypnotized and would have a certain relationship with the hypnotist – typically one of trust. Thus the might perform an act that was presented to them as overtly antisocial or criminal, knowing that in fact the care and humanity of the experimenting hypnotist would prevent any genuinely regrettable outcome. Over a period of years he utilized informal situations to try to persuade hypnotic subjects to commit genuine objectionable acts or crimes which were not so extreme as to be implausible.

To quote Erickson himself, 'The findings disclosed consistently the failure of all experimental measures to induce hypnotic subjects, in response to hypnotic suggestion, to perform acts of an objectionable character.' Erickson concluded: 'Hypnosis cannot be misused to induce hypnotized persons to commit actual wrongful acts, against themselves or others.'[6]

If hypnotic subjects are aware of the context in which they have been hypnotized in a laboratory, they will know at an unconscious level that any activity is 'just an experiment'. Erickson's findings indicate that without that safe context for 'approved' misbehaviour, subjects will not cooperate with a suggestion they deem immoral.

However, human beings do influence each other. We are all influencing each other all the time, because we are always communicating something in the non-verbal elements of our relationships. Certain groups have tried to take this to extremes using drugs, political rhetoric and techniques of situational distortion – in other words, brainwashing, the dictionary definition of which is 'to effect a radical change in the ideas and beliefs of a person by methods based on isolation, sleeplessness, hunger, extreme discomfort, pain and the alternation of kindness and cruelty.'

In the 1950s the CIA extensively experimented with mind-control techniques under the codename Operation Artichoke. One of their aims was 'to create a hypno-programmed robot assassin with no memory of his crime'.[7]

The late Dr William Bryan Jnr, who worked for the CIA for nearly ten years as their leading 'hypno-programmer', once made this statement:

> I am an expert in the use of hypnosis in criminal law . . . you have to have the person locked up physically, to have control over them, you have to use a certain amount of physical torture . . . and there is also the use of long-term hypnotic suggestion . . . probably drugs . . . whatever, and so on. Under these situations where you have all this going for you, like a prison camp and so on, yes, you can brainwash a person to do just about anything. What I am speaking about are the innumerable instances we ran into when I was running the country's brainwashing and anti-brainwashing programs.

So, hypnosis was one small part of a larger, coercive brainwashing programme.

One of the most famous cases involved Sirhan Sirhan, who assassinated Robert Kennedy. At his trial, psychiatrists testified that he was hypnotized at the time of the shooting and as a result remembered nothing of the event. Dr Eduard Simson-Kallas, his prison psychologist, described the court case as 'the psychiatric blunder of the century' and pleaded with the authorities to be allowed to de-programme Sirhan, but was refused. He told the *San Francisco Examiner* that 'Sirhan was hypnotically programmed'.

I have touched on this subject only briefly but if you would like to read more about the sensational side of hypnosis and mind control I recommend *Open to Suggestion* by Robert Temple, *Combatting Cult Mind Control* by Steve

Hassan, and Mrs Erickson's paper 'Observations Concerning Alterations in Hypnosis of Visual Perceptions'.[8]

## 13

# The Future

We live in a truly exciting time in our planet's history. These days there is more information to absorb and more to learn than ever before. We live in an information age. It looks as though the pace of change is going to get quicker and quicker, because the creative technology we have now is able to create more and better technology. You only have to look at how the exchange of information in the last hundred years has altered the world. A century ago the telegraph made it possible to send messages over great distances; by the turn of the century the wireless had arrived, followed shortly after by tape-recording, television and photocopying. The arrival of computers has made things both faster and more efficient as well.

As my friend Peter Russell says in his book *The White Hole in Time*, 'We can now communicate across the planet – mind to mind.' Something happens on one side of the world and we can watch it on our televisions seconds later, all sharing the experience. 'The eyes and ears of our telecommunications network are becoming the eyes and ears of humanity.'

Global communications systems can connect mind to

mind like nerve cells in a huge global brain. The complexity of this global network is doubling every two and a half years, and if it continues at its present rate it will equal the human brain in complexity by the year 2000.

Peter Russell also says, 'Mind has now become the dominant creative force on this planet.' Of course, the great thing about this is that we have all got one! Our thoughts are more powerful now than they have ever been, and with the exponential increases in technology we are likely to see some amazing changes within the next few years.

For example, in 1988 McGraw-Hill asked a cross-section of scientists for their technological predictions for the year 2000. Among the things they believe we will have are a cure for cancer, artificial eyesight for the blind, drugs to increase intelligence permanently, control of ageing and cryogenic preservation.

As well as these, who knows what virtual reality, fibre optics and genetic reprogramming will offer? The reason why this time in our history is so exciting is that we generally, unknowingly, stand poised to make an incredible leap in humanity's evolution. To do so we need a radical shift in values. Rather than continually looking for fulfilment in the outside world, which has made us overly competitive, we need to begin to find more contentment within, and I believe hypnosis is a powerful tool for bringing this about.

Many people resist change because they fear the unknown. The American economist Paul Zane Pilsner has some empowering concepts about the future and, in particular, wealth. Traditionally, economists studied the application of scarce resources. He argues that there is no scarcity, because with technology we are constantly able to do more with less.

What does all this have to do with hypnosis? One of Zane Pilsner's most interesting concepts is that these days a country's wealth is no longer gauged by its physical resources. If that was so, the former Soviet Union would be the richest country in the world, with all its oil, gold and raw minerals. Instead, these days it is technology, or ideas, that create wealth. The real wealth nowadays is in our thoughts, with the richest ideas creating the greatest wealth. Take computers. They are essentially made from sand, but the idea and thoughts behind them are genius. A major part of the Apple Corporation's success can be attributed to the idea of desk-top publishing, a concept that has sold millions of computers and continued the pace of technological change. Just think of it for a moment. You have got one of the richest and most powerful pieces of equipment in the world right between your ears – a brain!

As the saying goes, 'Invest in yourself.' There are so many activities these days in the area of personal development: yoga, Gestalt, meditation, stress management, Akido, NLP, massage – the list goes on. There are also some fabulous inventions being made all the time. Brain Machines: these comprise goggles with flashing LED lights that match your brain rhythms and alter your state. Float-ation tanks: although there are many variations of these, the basic principle is the same – a tank filled with about eight inches of salt water at body temperature in which you lie in darkness, isolated from the outside world. You have little external kinaesthetic awareness, no visual or auditory outside input, and so your awareness introverts and you can forget where you are, physically letting your mind take you on a journey. It is a perfect environment in which to begin vividly experiencing your imagination. You can also listen to hypnosis cassettes while floating, because you are in a profoundly altered state.

To me life is only as amazing as the ideas you have about it. By using self-hypnosis and operating my brain more efficiently as I have described in this book, I have been able to enjoy a much richer life than I had previously dreamed possible. I recommend you do the same – find the techniques that are most appealing and begin using them to create the kind of experiences you want to have.

**14**

# Hypno Facts

Hypnos is the Greek word for sleep.

The terms 'hypnotism', 'hypnotic' and 'hypnotist' were first used by the English surgeon James Braid in 1841 in his book entitled *Neurypnology*.

Every human being who is mentally sound can be hypnotized to some degree.

It is possible to hypnotize somebody over the telephone.

The Hindu Vedas, written around 1500 BC, mention the use of hypnotic-like techniques and procedures.

During the Middle Ages hypnosis was used by sorcerers and wizards, and flourished under the cloak of black magic.

Abyssinian fakirs used to use hypnosis on their slaves to make them more obedient.

In 1784 Louis XVI of France appointed a distinguished committee, including Benjamin Franklin, the American ambassador, Bailly, the astronomer, Lavoisier, the father of modern chemistry and Dr Guillotine, inventor of the guillotine, to investigate the healing powers of mesmerism.

Albert Einstein reckoned that humans use only about 10 per cent of their brains. While hypnotized, we can gain access to the other 90 per cent.

Carl Jung entered psychiatry as a result of reading a book by hypnotist Pierre Janet.

During the Second World War Winston Churchill would often have to stay up all night, so to avoid tiredness he would put himself into a trance by sitting in a chair and counting back in 3s, from 100 to 1.

Hypnosis was used successfully in both world wars to treat hundreds of men suffering from battle neuroses.

In the 1960s a Russian, Dr Raikov, managed to turn a number of ordinary citizens into fabulous painters and composers by using a hypnotic procedure.

In 1981 Sweden became the first country in the world to include hypnotic training in all the nation's schools.

Martin Reiser, director of the Behavioral Sciences Services for the Los Angeles Police Department, runs four-day courses for policemen on the use of hypnosis in crime.

Hypnosis has appeared in many literary works, the most notable being George du Maurier's 1894 work *Trilby*, in which the heroine falls under the spell of a villain named Svengali. Other famous writers who have used hypnosis as a theme include H. G. Wells, Sir Arthur Conan Doyle,

Edgar Allan Poe and John Buchan, but the most entertaining and successful novel, also made into a film, is probably Richard Condon's *The Manchurian Candidate*.

# Notes

## 2 WHAT IS HYPNOSIS?

1 Charles Baudouin, *Suggestion and Autosuggestion*, Allen and Unwin, 1920

2 Charles Baudouin, *The Inner Discipline*, Allen and Unwin, 1924

3 John Grinder and Richard Bandler, *TRANCE-formations*, Real People Press, USA, 1981

## 3 TRANCE INDUCTIONS

1 M. Argyle *et al.*, *British Journal of Social and Clinical Psychology*, 19, 1970, pp. 22–31

2 Harvey Mackay, *Beware the Naked Man Who Offers You His Shirt*, Piatkus Books, 1990

## 5 HYPNOTHERAPY

1 Dale Carnegie, *How to Stop Worrying and Start Living*, Cedar Books, 1948


## 8 MODERN HYPNOSIS

1 Jay Haley, *Uncommon Therapy: The Psychiatric Techniques of Milton H. Erickson, MD*, W. W. Norton and Co., USA 1973


## 10 THE NEW SCIENCE OF PERSONAL ACHIEVEMENT

1 Andrew Matthews, *Being Happy*, Media Masters Pte Ltd, 1988

2 Steven J. Sherman, 'The Self-Erasing Nature of Errors of Prediction', *Journal of Personality and Social Psychology*, 39, 1980, pp. 211–21


## 11 EVERYDAY HYPNOSIS

1 Smith and Engel, in Robert B. Cialdini, *Influence: Science and Practice*, Scott, Foresman, USA, 1988

2 Altheide and Johnson, in Robert B. Cialdini, *Influence: Science and Practice*, Scott, Foresman, USA, 1988

3 John Grinder and Richard Bandler, *TRANCE-formations*, Real People Press, USA, 1981

## 12 DANGERS AND ABUSES OF HYPNOSIS

1 Stanley Milgram, *Obedience to Authority*, Harper and Row, USA 1974

2 Gustav Le Bon, *The Crowd: A Study of the Popular Mind* (translated from *La psychologie des foules*, 1896), T. Fisher Unwin, thirteenth impression, 1921

3 Serge Moscovici, *The Age of the Crowd*, Cambridge University Press, 1985

4 Jeffrey Masson, *Against Therapy*, Collins, 1989

5 Andre Weitzenhoffer, 'The Production of Antisocial Acts under Hypnosis', *Journal of Abnormal Psychology*, 44, 1949, p. 421

6 Milton H. Erickson, *The Collected Papers of Milton H. Erickson*, Vol. 1, edited by Ernest L. Rossi, Irvington, USA, 1980, pp. 529, 530

7 *Secret History*, Exposed Films, Channel 4, in association with the Arts and Entertainments Network, 1992

8 Robert Temple, *Open to Suggestion*, The Aquarian Press, 1989; Steve Hassan, *Combatting Cult Mind Control*, The Aquarian Press, 1988; E. M. Erickson, 'Observations Concerning Alterations in Hypnosis of Visual Percep-

tions', in Milton H. Erickson, *The Collected Papers of Milton H. Erickson*, Vol. II, edited by Ernest L. Rossi, Irvington, USA, 1980

# Recommended Reading and Listening

These are the works that I have found both impressive and helpful. Some of the authors and books or tapes have already been mentioned, but here is the list in full.


## GENERAL

Richard Bach, *Jonathan Livingstone Seagull*, Pan, 1973
   – *Illusions*, Pan, 1979
   – *Bridge Across Forever*, Pan, 1985

Eric Berne, *The Games People Play*, Penguin, 1970

Robert B. Cialdini, *Influence: Science and Practice* (second edition), Scott, Foresman, USA, 1988

Louise Hay, *You Can Heal Your Life*, Eden Grove Editions, 1988

Napoleon Hill, *Think and Grow Rich*, Fawcett, USA, 1987

Philip Kapleau, *Zen: Dawn in the West*, Rider, 1980

Dr James E. Loehr and Peter J. McLaughlin, *Mental Toughness* (tapes)

Maxwell Maltz, *Psycho-Cybernetics and Self-fulfilment*, Bantam Books/published by arrangement with Grosset & Dunlap Inc., USA, 1970

Andrew Matthews, *Being Happy*, Media Masters Pte Ltd, 1988

C. W. Metcalf, *Humor, Risk and Change* (video and audio)
    You can contact him at:
    2801 South Remington, Suite 2
    Fort Collins, Colorado
    CO 80525, USA
    Tel: 010–1–303–226–0610

Paraliminal Tapes, *Holiday Cheer*
   *Instantaneous Personal Magnetism*
   *Memory Supercharger*
   *Personal Genius*
   *Prosperity*
   *Self-Esteem Supercharger*
    Address:
    Leavning Strategies Corporation
    900 East Wayzata Boulevard
    Suite M 310
    Wayzata
    Minnesota 55391–1857
    USA

Anthony Robbins, *Personal Power* (tape series)

*– Unlimited Power*, Fawcett, USA, 1987
*– Awaken the Giant*, Summit Books, USA, 1991

Peter Russell, *The White Hole in Time*, Aquarian Press/ Thorsons, 1992

Chet B. Snow, *Dreams of the Future*, Aquarian Press, 1991

Chuck Spezzano, *Awaken the Gods*, Wellspring Publications, 1991

I also recommend doing his workshops on Relationships and Master.
    You can obtain details from:
    The Leadership Network
    75 Fifth Avenue
    London W10 4DW

Alan Watts, *The Way of Zen*, Penguin, 1990

Stuart Wilde, *Affirmations*, White Dove International, USA, 1987


## ERICKSON BOOKS

Richard Bandler and John Grinder, *Patterns of the Hypnotic Techniques of Milton H. Erickson, MD*, Vol. 1, Meta Publications, USA, 19745

Milton H. Erickson, *The Collected Papers of Milton H. Erickson on Hypnosis*, Vols. 1–4, edited by Ernest L. Rossi, Irvington, USA, 1980

Milton H. Erickson *et al.*, *Hypnotic Realities: The Induction of Clinical Hypnosis and Forms of Indirect Suggestion*, Irvington, USA, 1976

David Gordon and Maribeth Meyers-Anderson, *Phoenix: The Therapeutic Patterns of Milton H. Erickson*, Meta Publications, USA, 1981

Jay Haley, *Uncommon Therapy: The Psychiatric Techniques of Milton H. Erickson, MD*, W. W. Norton and Co., USA, 1973

Sidney Rosen, *My Voice Will Go with You: Teaching Tales of Milton H. Erickson*, W. W. Norton and Co., USA, 1983

## NEURO-LINGUISTIC PROGRAMMING

Richard Bandler, *Using Your Brain for a Change*, Real People Press, USA, 1985

Richard Bandler and John Grinder, *Reframing: Neuro-Linguistic Programming and the Transformation of Meaning*, Real People Press, USA, 1982

Charles Faulkner, *Metaphors of Identity* (tapes)

Byron A. Lewis and Frank Pucelik, *Magic of NLP Demystified: A Pragmatic Guide to Communication and Change*, Metamorphous Press, USA, 1990

Donald J. Moine and John H. Herd, *Modern Persuasion*

*Strategies: The Hidden Advantage in Selling*, Pfeifer-Hamilton, USA, 1984

Jerry Richardson, *The Magic of Rapport: How You Can Gain Personal Power in Any Situation*, Meta Publications, USA, 1988

John Seymour and Joseph O'Connor, *Introducing Neuro-Linguistic Programming: The New Psychology of Personal Excellence*, Thorsons SF, USA, 1990


## HYPNOSIS


Richard Bandler and John Grinder, *TRANCE-formations*, Real People Press, USA, 1981

Pierre Clement, *Hypnosis and Power Learning*, Westwood Publishing Co., USA, 1979

D. Corydon Hammond *et al.*, *Handbook of Hypnotic Suggestions and Metaphors*, W. W. Norton and Co., USA, 1990

Steven Heller, *Monsters & Magical Sticks, or There's No Such Thing As Hypnosis*, New Falcon Publications, USA, 1987

Charles Tebbets, *Self-Hypnosis and Other Mind Expanding Techniques*, Borden, USA, 1977

Stephen Wolinsky and Margaret O. Ryan, *Trances People Live: Healing Approaches in Quantum Psychology*, Bramble Co., USA, 1991

Pam Young, *Personal Change Through Self Hypnosis*, Angus and Robertson, 1986

If, after having read this book, you are interested in becoming a hypnotherapist, there are many courses around that may well give you some letters after your name. Remember, though, that some are much better than others. I personally recommend the UK Training College, which runs a superb course. You can write for information to the Principal, Mandy Langford, at:

St Charles Hospital
Exmoor Street
London W10 6DZ

Or telephone 081 964 1206.

*faber and faber*

# The Paranormal World of Paul McKenna

Is it real because you believe it, or do you believe it because it is real? Paul McKenna, television's hypnotic genius, takes us on an extraordinary tour of the paranormal.

He investigates real life X Files – cases of UFOs, Extraterrestrials and Ghosts, and redraws the boundaries of what is scientifically 'impossible'.

The phenomena explored in this book will challenge the way you think.

*faber and faber*

# Paul McKenna

Please send me:

\_\_\_\_ copies of **The Paranormal World of Paul McKenna**

(0 571 19245 9) £5.99 each

I enclose a cheque for £ _____

made payable to Faber and Faber Ltd.

Please charge my:

Access / Visa / Amex / Diner's Club / Eurocard / Switch

(Switch Issue Number \_\_\_\_\_ )

Name of Cardholder _____ Expiry Date: _____

Account Number:

☐ ☐ ☐ ☐ ☐ ☐ ☐ ☐ ☐ ☐ ☐ ☐ ☐ ☐ ☐ ☐

Name _____

Address _____

Signed _____Date _____

Send to:

Faber Book Services,

Burnt Mill, Elizabeth Way, Harlow, Essex CM20 2HX

Tel 01279 417134  Fax 01279 417366

# Index